# VOCATIONS AND FUTURE CHURCH LEADERSHIP

National
Conference
of Catholic
Bishops

The
Collegeville
Papers
June 9-16,
1986

*Vocations and Future Church Leadership* presents the addresses delivered at the Bishop's Assembly for Prayer and Reflection on Vocations held at St. John's University, Collegeville, Minnesota, June 9–16, 1986. The addresses were edited by staff for the Assembly Planning Committee, approved by the respective authors, and authorized for publication by the undersigned.

Monsignor Daniel F. Hoye
General Secretary
August 29, 1986                                          NCCB/USCC

Cover illustration:
St. John's Campus, Collegeville, Minnesota, 1886

Excerpts from *The Documents of Vatican II*, Walter M. Abbott, SJ, General Editor, copyright © 1966, America Press, Inc., 106 West 56th Street, New York, NY 10019, are reprinted with permission. All rights reserved.

Scripture texts used in this work are taken from *The New American Bible*, copyright © 1970, by the Confraternity of Christian Doctrine, Washington, D.C., and are used by permission of the copyright owner. All rights reserved.

ISBN 1-55586-108-3

Copyright © 1986
United States Catholic Conference, Inc.
1312 Massachusetts Avenue, N.W.
Washington, D.C. 20005-4105
All rights reserved.

# CONTENTS

# PREFACE

The Catholic bishops of the United States gathered at St. John's University in Collegeville, Minnesota June 9–16, 1986, to discuss and reflect on vocations and church leadership. The aim of this special assembly was affective rather than effective; the bishops had no intention of devising new vocations programs. They met to get to know one another better, to build community, and to develop a collective sense of where they stand as regards vocations and the future leadership needs of the Church. Nevertheless, their reflections can hardly fail to influence policy at the diocesan and national levels and are, therefore, of considerable interest.

The choice of topic for the assembly needs little explanation. Pope John Paul II has called vocations to the priesthood and religious life "the fundamental problem of the Church." While the growing shortage of clergy and of men and women religious is not as noticeable in this country as elsewhere, millions of American Catholics have begun to feel its effects and millions more soon will.

In 1960, the Catholic population of the United States was about 40 million. There were 53,000 priests, 168,000 sisters, 10,500 brothers, and about 45,000 seminarians. In 1983, the Catholic population was 52 million, and there were 58,000 priests, 121,000 sisters, 7,500 brothers, and 12,000 seminarians. Moreover, the median age of priests in 1980 was about 52 years, that of sisters about 59 years.[1] Experts estimate that only about one-half as many priests will be available for pastoral work in 1990 as were available a decade before.

Quite without exaggeration, the "vocations crisis" is changing the face of American Catholicism. Parishes close or are consolidated because there is no priest to serve them. Women religious, permanent deacons, even lay people are assigned to administer other "priestless" parishes. Tuition in parochial schools soars as women religious retire and full-salaried lay faculty replace them. Leadership in the Church, once primarily the responsibility of priests and religious, falls increasingly to an unprepared laity.

Under the circumstances, the bishops' deliberations at St. John's had an air of urgency. They heard eight presentations on various aspects of the vocations picture and discussed each at length. These talks, modified slightly to accommodate the shift from podium to printed page, are reproduced here. Taken together, they present a fair cross section of the bishops' reflections—both positive and negative—on the current state of vocations and some indication as to what direction they might take in dealing with the crisis.

Archbishop Pio Laghi opened the assembly with a discussion of Pope John Paul II's recent addresses on vocations. He also read a message from the Holy Father (here printed separately).

Following a day of recollection, Bernard Cardinal Law offered the bishops a broad Christian anthropology in which to situate a discussion of vocations. "The human vocation," he said, "is most radically . . . a call to experience and live life as pure gift, as a gift of self, as sacrificial love. Christ is our vocation. His sacrificial love is the revelation of the human vocation." Summing up, he remarked: "The 'crisis of vocation' is to be seen for what it is: a crisis of faith, a crisis of our call to holiness."

Bishop Raymond Lucker spoke on the vocation of the laity. Recalling that every Christian has a vocation by reason of baptism, the bishop said that "there is no shortage in the call of the Spirit to extend the kingdom of God." Bishop Lucker

---

1. Data on Catholic population and on priests, sisters, and brothers from National Conference of Catholic Bishops, *Catholic Church Personnel in the United States* (Washington, D.C.: NCCB, 1984), 4–5, 7, 13. Data on seminarians from National Conference of Catholic Bishops, *Laborers for the Vineyard* (Washington, D.C.: USCC Office of Publishing and Promotion Services, 1984), 7.

laid special stress on the laity's call to sanctify the world. "Parishes will be strong when people feel and see the connection between faith and work, between Sunday morning liturgy and Monday morning work, between seeing God's presence at the altar and seeing him at the clinic, the desk, the farm, and the sink."

Bishop Lawrence Welsh of Spokane, chairman of the Bishops' Committee on Vocations, summarized current research on vocations and offered a number of recommendations for the future.

Bishop J. Terry Steib, SVD, delivered the talk on vocations to the religious life that ailing Bishop Joseph Francis, SVD, had prepared. The address emphasized the changes religious congregations have witnessed in recent years and declared that these congregations are looking for candidates willing to take "apostolic risks."

Archbishop Daniel Pilarczyk's presentation on vocations to the ordained ministry brought a standing ovation. Noting the great shift that has taken place in the priest's role in the Church, Archbishop Pilarczyk said that the modern pastor must "[be] a good shepherd without treating the people like sheep, [be] a loving father without treating the people like children." He devoted a good portion of his talk to celibacy, saying that "there is no essential, inherent connection between priesthood and celibacy that would make their separation absurd." However, he described celibates as "people who are so enchanted, so fascinated by Christ and his kingdom, so caught up in their spell, that they do not want to do anything else. . . . They want their lives to be completely available for apostolic service."

Joseph Cardinal Bernardin spoke on the final day, giving his impressions of the preceding talks and the discussion they provoked. His closing words capture the optimistic spirit that dominated the last few days of the assembly. "As we discuss vocations, surely we must identify and address the problems if they are to be resolved. But, let's not become captives of the problems. . . . I am convinced that there are many who will respond if we invite them. So, let's go about our task with enthusiasm and confidence."

David M. Byers
Editor

# A MESSAGE FROM HIS HOLINESS POPE JOHN PAUL II

*To My Venerable Brothers,*
*The Bishops of the United States of America*

On the occasion of your meeting in Collegeville, Minnesota, I wish to assure you of my spiritual closeness to you and of my prayerful support for your pastoral initiative. You are assembling in a spirit of collegial responsibility to reflect on the vital subject of vocations for your local Churches.

Your reflections on vocations to the priesthood and religious life are being linked with reflections on the need for all the members of the Church to be conscious of their common calling to live the gospel message and to build up the Body of Christ.

It is indeed fitting to emphasize over and over again the universal vocation to holiness of the whole People of God. It is truly opportune to proclaim with insistence the need for all the faithful to be aware of the precise responsibilities that derive from their baptism and confirmation. In this regard, the Second Vatican Council says explicitly that the laity "are assigned to the apostolate by the Lord himself" (*Apostolicam Actuositatem* [=AA], 3).

A keen realization of their Christian dignity is a great in-

1

centive to all the People of God to fulfill their sacred role in worship, Christian living, evangelization, and human advancement. As pastors of the flock, it is our responsibility to encourage all our brothers and sisters in the faith to live a life worthy of the calling that they have received (cf. Eph 4:1). It is our task to assure them of their shared responsibility for the Gospel of our Lord Jesus Christ and, at the same time, to encourage them in their individual contributions to the Church and to the whole of society. These individual contributions are expressive of the rich variety characteristic of the Body of Christ.

One of the great tasks of all Catholics is to help foster those conditions in the community that will facilitate individuals and social Christian living. Only if the faithful are responding to their personal Christian vocation will the community be sustained in its respect and love for Christian marriage and for the priesthood and religious life.

An integral part of Christian family life is the inculcation in its members of an appreciation of the priesthood and religious life in relation to the whole of the Church. Our common pastoral experience confirms the fact that there is a very special need in the Church today to promote vocations to the priesthood and to religious life. It also confirms the fact that generous and persevering efforts made in inviting young people to respond to these vocations have been rewarded. I know that in your deliberations, you will discuss appropriate ways that this can be ever more effectively accomplished. The correlation of your varied pastoral experiences will undoubtedly assist you greatly in planning for the future.

On my part, I would like to emphasize above all the general attitude toward vocations to be cultivated within ourselves and to be shared with the clergy and faithful. In this regard, it is necessary to foster profound trust in the power of the Paschal Mystery as the perennial source of vocations to the priesthood and religious life. In every age, the Church not only reiterates her esteem for these vocations but she acknowledges their unique and irreplaceable character. She, likewise, expresses the profound conviction that the Lord, who wills them for his Church, is ever active in calling young people to fulfill his will.

The Church's earnestness in promoting vocations to the priesthood and religious life is explained by her desire to be faithful to God's will to maintain both the hierarchical structure of his Church and the state of religious life. The Church

2

extols and promotes the special consecration proper to both of these vocations, even if a certain number of functions exercised by priests and religious are shared increasingly by the laity.

Dear Brothers: In union with the whole Church, let us face the vocations challenge with that equanimity and realism that take into account the effectiveness of prayer and that are never devoid of supernatural hope. Let us proclaim forcefully the power of the Risen Christ to continue to draw young people to himself in every age of the Church and, therefore, in our own. Let us look to the Paschal Mystery as the inexhaustible source of strength for young people to follow Christ with generosity and sacrifice, in chastity, poverty, and obedience, and in perfect charity.

The Church cannot exempt herself from utilizing every worthy means to attract vocations, including proper publicity and personal example. Yet, she unhesitatingly proclaims that her strength comes only from the Lord. It is he alone who gives vocations and the grace to accept them and to overcome obstacles to them.

In the assemblies of the faithful, let us invoke the Lord's promise to be with his Church until the end of time (cf. Mt 28:20). We must encourage our people to express their hope in prayer. In acknowledging the Lord's fidelity in providing for the needs of his Spouse, the Church, we offer a hymn of praise to the Lamb of God who was slain—to him who died but now lives for ever and ever.

We find in the precious blood of the crucified and risen Savior the strength to sustain every vocation that God gives to his Church. "To him whose power now at work in us can do immeasurably more than we ask or imagine—to him be glory in the Church and in Christ Jesus through all generations, world without end. Amen" (Eph 3:20).

*Joannes Paulus PP. II*

Vatican City
May 14, 1986

3

# POPE JOHN PAUL II
# AND THE PROBLEM OF
# VOCATIONS

## Archbishop Pio Laghi
## Apostolic Pro-Nuncio

Let me begin by expressing my gratitude to Bishop Malone and to all of you for your gracious invitation to address this assembly on behalf of the Holy Father. We are here to deal with a topic whose importance can readily be understood by the fact that you, the bishops of the United States, are devoting an entire week to a prayerful discussion of the problem of vocations in today's world.

I base my address on what Pope John Paul II has stated on the subject of vocations during these almost eight years of his pontificate. More specific, I have chosen to pass in review the special messages given by the Holy Father on the annual occasion of the World Day of Prayer for Vocations. You are aware, of course, that it was the late Pope Paul VI who inaugurated the practice of holding a special Day of Prayer for Vocations. In 1964, during the Second Vatican Council, Pope Paul VI established that this observance would take place each year on the Fourth Sunday of Easter. Appropriately enough, the gospel reading for that day is a passage from John in which

Jesus speaks about the Good Shepherd. Pope John Paul II has continued the initiative of Pope Paul VI and each year has sought to focus on different aspects of the vocations question.

In his very first message for the Day of Prayer, the Holy Father proposed three key words that, in a sense, capture the whole issue of vocations. These words were *pray, call,* and *respond.* The reason why we *pray* for vocations is obvious; Christ himself commanded us to do so: "Pray, therefore, the Lord of the harvest to send out laborers into his harvest" (Mt 9:38). That there is a need to *call* laborers into the harvest is again evidenced by the fact that Christ too called his disciples to accompany him: "Follow me and I will make you fishers of men" (Mt 4:19). It would appear to follow that the task of praying for vocations and calling candidates to the ministry lies principally with those who have already responded to that invitation. The obligation to *respond,* on the other hand, falls upon those to whom the invitation has been given.

The Holy Father recalls for us some of the various responses to God's call that are found in the Scriptures. He refers, first of all, to the response of Peter and Andrew: "Immediately they left their nets and followed him" (Mt 4:20); then, to that of Levi the Publican: "And he left everything, and rose and followed him" (Lk 5:28); the response of Simon Peter, spokesman for the Twelve: "Lord, to whom shall we go? You have the words of eternal life" (Jn 6:68). From the very earliest proclamation of the Gospel, right up to the present, countless men and women have given their personal response, their free and deliberate response, to the call of Christ. They have chosen the priesthood, the religious life, life in the missions, as the reason for and the ideal of existence.

In his message for the seventeenth Day of Prayer in 1980, Pope John Paul II made a very direct appeal to bishops, priests, deacons, and religious worldwide: "Evangelize in an ever more intense and effective way the People of God, especially the families and the young people, concerning the holy truths about the priesthood, the missions, the consecrated life. The People of God, when it prays for vocation, must know well why it is praying and for whom." You can sense how serious the pope is when he asks us to speak to the issue of vocations. He goes on to state that "the faithful, families, young people must realize ever more clearly that the Church and her priests, missionaries, and other consecrated persons do not take their origin solely from human causes or motives or interests, but from the merciful design of God. . . ."

6

The conclusion of the 1980 message is virtually a litany of prayer for vocations. Prayer was the first of the pontiff's key words, and in this message he truly teaches us how to pray.

As a starting point for his 1981 message, the Holy Father mentions that later in the year there will be an International Congress that will discuss the pastoral care of vocations. The theme of the congress was "Local Churches and Vocations." Thus, the pope turns his attention to the local Churches and notes that "every local Church must become ever more clearly aware of what it is, in the light of the mystery of the universal Church. For it is in this light of faith that the local Church finds the strength to live, strive and grow. . . ."

Pope John Paul II adds: "There must be clear understanding of the *nature* of the vocation and mission of the People of God, as it travels through the world towards its eternal homeland. There must be equally clear understanding of the *identity* of the bishop, the priest, and the deacon; of the nature of their precise and irreplaceable mission at the service of the People of God; and of what distinguishes these persons, who have been consecrated through Holy Orders, from the other members of the People of God. There must be understanding, with no less clarity, of the identity and activity of the other men and women who are also consecrated, not through Holy Orders but through religious vows or other forms of religious commitment, to the service of the People of God. This clearer understanding, in the light of faith, will impel us to thank and praise the Lord for the abundance of ministries and gifts with which he has enriched his Church. And it will also be very useful in helping each member of the Church to reflect on his or her personal responsibilities, to discover his or her own personal vocation, and to be ready to serve the ecclesial community generously with the power and grace of the Holy Spirit."

Many of you have far greater practical, pastoral experience than do I in fostering vocations. I believe, however, that it is essential for us to turn directly to *families*, in order to educate them to the point where the vocations that certainly exist are nurtured properly by the family.

In his 1982 message, Pope John Paul II made a direct appeal to Christian families. He asked all believing families to reflect upon the mission they have received from God for the education of their children in the faith and in Christian living. It is a mission, the Holy Father asserted, that also involves responsibilities with regards to their children's vocations. Quoting the Second Vatican Council, the Holy Father reminded parents that "the education of children should be such that when they grow up they will be able to follow their vocation, including a religious vocation, and choose their state in life with full consciousness of responsibility" (*Gaudium et Spes* [=GS], 52). Cooperation between families and the Church for vocations has deep roots in the mystery and the "ministry" of the Christian family. The pope refers to *Familiaris Consortio:* "Indeed, the family that is open to transcendent values, that serves its brothers and sisters with joy, that fulfills its duties with generous fidelity and is aware of its daily sharing in the mystery of the glorious cross of Christ, becomes the primary and most excellent seedbed of vocations to a life of consecration to the kingdom of God" (53).

For the celebration of the twentieth Day of Prayer for Vocations, the Holy Father wished to emphasize four key points and offered a summary of his thoughts on each.

1. *The Word of God and Vocations.* Vocations to the priesthood and the consecrated life exist in and for the Church in accordance with God's plan, which in his love he has willed to reveal to us. Therefore, they exist for a specific mission of their own, which is not to be confused with any other purely human ideal, however noble.

2. *Prayer and Vocations.* The Church is a gift of God for the salvation of humanity. Therefore, vocations to the total service of the Church are also a special gift of God. For this reason we ask this gift from him alone, for he alone can give it. We ask for it with our hearts open to the world, looking to the good of all humanity. Remember that the Lord Jesus has invited us to pray for vocations, precisely because his merciful heart saw the world's suffering.

3. *Witness and Vocations.* You are familiar with these words of the Council: "The duty of fostering vocations falls on the whole Christian community, and they should discharge it principally by living full Christian lives" (*Optatam Totius* [=OT] 2). The Lord Jesus had spoken of the "good soil" that brought forth grain, some a hundredfold, some sixty, some thirty" (Mt 18:18). Where there is faith, prayer, love, apostolate, and Christian living, there the gifts of God abound.

4. *A Personal Call and Vocations.* God calls whom he wishes out of the free initiative of his love. But, he also wishes to call *through* us. This is how the Lord Jesus acted. It was Andrew who brought to him his brother Peter. Jesus called Philip, but it was Philip who called Nathanael. One should

not fear to suggest directly to young or not so young persons the call of the Lord.

As I noted earlier, the Gospel for the Fourth Sunday of Easter is that of the Good Shepherd. In his 1984 message, Pope John Paul II, pastor of the Universal Church, addressed these words to the world's shepherds: "To you, revered brothers in the episcopate, who, in imitation of the Good Shepherd, guide with love and trepidation the flock that has been entrusted to you, is joined my gratitude and that of the Church for the exemplary efforts that you undertake in your communities to foster all consecrated vocations. Tangible evidence of them are the programs and plans of diocesan action, which you have published or which you are preparing. . . . The Lord is giving to the Church a new fruitfulness in the field of vocations. Especially, in some countries, a prominent increase is being manifested, for which one will never be thankful enough for the goodness of God. These signs of hope will stimulate you to persevere with courage and fervor in such a precious work." These are words filled with hope.

The United Nations proclaimed 1985 "International Youth Year." The Holy Father focused his thoughts on the world's young people in his message on vocations for that year. But, he also had a word of advice to bishops in this regard. "To serve the young is to serve the Church," he reminded us. Indeed, he went on to state that this service to the young is a task to which other tasks must be subordinated and directed. One of the suggestions Pope John Paul II made on this subject is particularly important: It is necessary for us *to go* to the young because they will not come to us spontaneously. It is incumbent upon us to find ways to attract the young and to convey to them the Lord's message in understandable terms.

For this year's message, the Holy Father chose to highlight the role of parishes in the development and promotion of vocations. He set down several conditions required for effective growth in vocations. The parish must be "a vibrant community . . . , a praying community . . . , an inviting community . . . , a missionary community. In the pope's thinking, "a community without vocations is like a family without children."

Up to this point, I have spoken about the Holy Father's thoughts on vocations as expressed in his annual messages. Now, I would like to reflect on how he perceives his own call to the priesthood. In Andre Frossard's interview with the pope, entitled *Non Abbiate Paura*, the Holy Father spoke about his own vocation in these words: "Toward the end of my studies at the Lyceum, those who were around me thought that I would have chosen the priesthood. I myself did not think so. I was sure I would remain a layman, though an active one in the life of the Church, but certainly not a priest." The Holy Father added: "After the death of my father in February 1941, little by little I became aware of my true route. I was working in a factory and, to the extent possible during that fearful period of wartime occupation, I dedicated myself to my passion for literature and drama. My vocation to the priesthood took hold while I was in the middle of all that. The following year, in the fall, I knew that I was called. I saw clearly that which I would have to leave behind and the goal I would have to reach without looking back. I would become a priest. . . . In October 1942, I became one of the students at the clandestine seminary attached to the theology faculty of the Jagellonian University, which operated secretly at the time of the occupation. I prepared for examinations during my free hours and even during breaks from work at the factory."

The Holy Father then recalled for Mr. Frossard the various friendships that contributed to his vocation to the priesthood. "It was my confessor who perceived exactly the right moment to tell me that Christ was calling me to his priesthood. My gratitude and recognition goes also to my educators in the seminary, to my theology professors, and to the priests who were my colleagues during my brief assignment in a parish. I am particularly indebted to one of these priests. I cannot forget to mention Cardinal Sapieha, my bishop, who during the war and the terrible occupation proved to be an authentic patriot."

The Holy Father speaks also of numerous lay friends who had an influence on his decision to be a priest. He singles out one man in particular, a tailor by trade, whose name was John and who first introduced Karol Wojtyla to the writings of St. John of the Cross. Besides St. John, two other saints played a significant role in his priestly formation: St. Francis of Assisi and St. John Vianney. Interestingly, only the last of these holy men was a priest. In speaking about St. Francis, the pope notes that the saint gave his very soul to God and he asks: "What is a priestly vocation if not a call to give one's soul?"

These intimate thoughts of Pope John Paul II compel us to recognize how marvelously God chooses various instruments to reach into the depths of a person whom he is calling to his special service.

Allow me to bring my reflections to a close with a prayer for vocations composed by the Holy Father:

O Jesus, our Good Shepherd,
     bless all our parishes with numerous priests,
     deacons, men and women in religious life,
     consecrated laity and missionaries,
     according to the needs of the entire world,
     which You love and wish to save.

We especially entrust our community to You;
     grant us the spirit of the first Christians
     so that we may be a cenacle of prayer,
     in loving acceptance of the Holy Spirit
     and his gifts.

Assist our pastors and all who live
     a consecrated life.
Guide the steps of those who have responded
     generously to your call and are preparing
     to receive Holy Orders or to profess
     the evangelical counsels.

Look with love on so many well-disposed young people
     and call them to follow You.
Help them to understand that in You alone
     can they attain to complete fulfillment.

To this end we call on the powerful intercession of
     Mary, Mother and Model of all vocations.
We beseech You to sustain our faith
     with the certainty that the Father will grant
     what You have commanded us to ask.

Amen.

# THE MYSTERY OF VOCATION

## Bernard Cardinal Law
## Archbishop of Boston

To think "vocation" is to invite the word *crisis*. However different the picture in India, Africa, Poland, or the Philippines, for us—or at least for me—the word connotes a problem.

In slightly more than two weeks the Archdiocese of Boston has buried three priests, each in his fifties, each active at the time of sudden death: two were pastors, the third was a seminary professor. This sobering triad has rendered yet more severe the statistic of fifty-plus openings for priests, according to our present criteria for staffing. To play it out further, I ordained only eleven priests last Saturday. Obviously, the staffing criteria can be changed; obviously, the seventeen ordinations to the permanent diaconate must be taken into account; obviously, the moment invites the Church to live out more fully and effectively her self-understanding as a priestly people, each one called to share in mission. Yet, granted all of this, we face a serious crisis.

I believe this crisis affords us a providential opportunity to understand better God's plan of creation and redemption, to discern his will and respond to it with ever growing determination, confidence, and joy. However, this will not be possible unless we seek to penetrate as deeply as possible the roots of our present situation. We will have the opportunity to reflect on the different vocations to which the Lord calls men and women for service to his Church and humankind. I see it as my task to invite a meditation on vocations in a more generic way. My plan is to reflect on what a vocation means in the most fundamental way possible. I think this should be our starting point.

Put in technical terms, we need to reflect on vocation in the context of a Christian anthropology, that is, in the context of our understanding of what it means to be a human person as revealed fully in the mystery of the Incarnate Word (cf. GS, 22). Unless we do this, we can be paralyzed in our own vocation as bishops either by a pessimism produced by grim statistics, or by a misplaced optimism that imagines that things will get better when we move out of this "time of transition." It is not statistics or any sociological analysis (pessimistic or optimistic) that will lead us to an understanding of the mystery of vocation. It is our prayerful reflection on what a vocation is according to God's creative and redemptive wisdom that will disclose to us the truth.

I am convinced that we need to back away a moment from specific vocations and reflect on what they all have in common. Accordingly, we shall ask ourselves first: what is a vocation? What does it tell us about what a human person is meant to be? We will see that vocation is an essential element of our existence as persons. Therefore, it is only the mystery of Christ that will disclose to us the full truth about vocation. Our knowledge of what a human being is comes from our knowledge of the mystery of Christ. Our anthropology, although it contains truths accessible to nonbelievers, is derived from our Christology. No other way is possible for us.

From this perspective, we shall discover behind the negative cultural forces militating against vocations the horror of sin. Sin is the refusal of vocation. Our "vocation crisis" reflects the inroads made by sin in the hierarchy of values, the accepted customs, and the standards that characterize so much of our cultural milieu. The vocation crisis can be overcome only to the degree that we respond to the way of redemption revealed through Christ Jesus. There is no other way out of our dilemma except faith in Christ crucified and risen, and what this faith tells us about the redemption of vocation.

In this, as in all difficulties we experience in the life of the Church, it is not simply a matter of finding a solution to problems. It is a matter of responding faithfully to what the Lord's saving death and resurrection require and empower us to do. The "vocation crisis" betokens the need for redemption at the most fundamental level of human existence. Unless we see it this way, we will be deceived about what has happened and is happening to us. We are, therefore, called to strengthen our resolve as bishops to be the ever more faithful custodians and ministers of the sacred mysteries of our redemption.

We always have as our most sure guide the one in whom our redemption has already been fully manifested. Therefore, to end this reflection, we shall turn to Mary to learn from her the truth about the fulfillment of the human vocation, as we implore her help in offering to the Church and our world a clear vision of redeemed humanity's vocation.

# VOCATION AND HUMAN PERSONHOOD

What is a vocation? Better still, What does the experience of vocation tell us about what it means to be a human person?

Vocation means a calling. To be conscious of a vocation is to be aware of being summoned by name, by someone. A vocation is an appeal from a person to a person. A vocation is a call that makes the one who calls present to the one called. A vocation is the expression, manifestation, projection, appearance of "another someone" who has come outside of his or her inner self toward me. He or she has committed him or herself to me, put his or herself in my hands, so to speak, and awaits a similar response. My vocation is that response; it is that equal commitment of my innermost self to the one who calls. A vocation is thus always "other-directed." It is a self-giving responding to another self-giving.

Our self-giving must be to another person who has value for his or her own sake (cf. GS, 24). Anything else is a diminishment of the dignity of the person, of the transcendence of the person. That is why a true vocation always seeks to establish a communion of persons. Moreover, that is why every authentic vocation is unreserved and permanent. A true personal self-giving cannot be otherwise. I cannot split my identity as myself!

Therefore, the experience of vocation is equivalent to the experience of personhood. Through it, two central anthropological insights emerge. In the words of the Second Vatican Council: "Man is the only creature on earth that God wanted for its own sake" (GS, 24). That is the first insight: human personal existence has a value that depends on nothing whatsoever other than itself. It is not worthy of persons to make themselves or others instruments of anything or anyone. In

15

short, personal existence is a pure gift to be accepted and respected as such. The fundamental vocation is the vocation to life as pure gift, the call to existence out of nonexistence.

The second anthropological principle is a consequence of our experience of the call to existence as pure gift. Again, in the words of Vatican II: "Man can fully discover his true self only in a sincere giving of himself" (GS, 24). In his most recent encyclical on the Holy Spirit, Pope John Paul II says that this conciliar text "can be said to sum up the whole of Christian anthropology" (cf. *Dominum et Vivificantem* [=DV], 59). The experience of the fundamental vocation to existence as pure gift leads simultaneously to the experience of the fullness of existence as thanksgiving, as a sincere giving of self as gift. But, why is this called a Christian anthropology? This brings us to the second part of our reflection: Christ our vocation.

# CHRIST OUR VOCATION

To repeat: The mystery of the Incarnate Word provides us with the fullest disclosure of what it means to be a human being. It is in the truth about Christ that we discover most fully the truth about the human person. We must be firmly convinced of this. The truth about Christ is not something "added" to what we can otherwise discover about the meaning of human life. It is the truth about human life disclosed simultaneously with, and inseparably from, the truth about God—more specific, about a trinitarian God, about "the mystery of the Father and of his love" as Vatican II stated it (cf. GS, 22). We cannot overestimate the value of this teaching. Bluntly, without Christ, we cannot know with certainty and fully what it means to be a human person; we cannot understand fully the human vocation to existence as such.

Christ is the "new Adam" of which the first Adam was a "type." The creation of the human being in Christ, with Christ as the blueprint, so to speak, is of course a teaching firmly based in Scripture and the fathers (cf. Rom 5:14). Christ is our vocation as human beings. He is the model or goal that we are called to follow in God's plan of creation and redemption. We are being "formed into Christ"; we reach "full maturity" in Christ! As the "image of the invisible God," he reveals the mystery of the triune God in which he, the Second Person of the Most Holy Trinity, is the One eternally called, and the One eternally responding. His very identity is vocation. As the Incarnate Word, as the new Adam, he is given to us as our vocation. He is the Father's call to us by the power of the Spirit. The vocation of every single man and woman is Christ.

What does Christ our vocation tell us about our vocation to existence as human beings? How does that primordial vocation show us that "man can fully discover his true self only by a sincere giving of himself?"

St. Paul writes to the Philippians: "Your attitude must be that of Christ. . . . Though he was in the form of God, he did not deem equality with God as something to be grasped at" (Phil 2:5–6). Some commentators see in this a reference to Adam, to man as created in the beginning. Though created in the image and likeness of God, Adam, deceived by the serpent, sought to grasp divinity by turning against God. He ceased to experience human existence as pure gift. He thus denied the truth about his own self; he wounded, distorted, rejected his own humanity. Now, the second Adam restores to us the perception that Adam had lost. He discloses the full truth about the human vocation. He does this through the cross and resurrection.

Thus, St. Paul continues: "Rather, he emptied himself . . . obediently accepting death, death on a cross" (Phil 2:7–8). The human vocation is one of sacrificial love, of total, unreserved, permanent self-giving. Thus, it is that "man can only discover his true self by a sincere giving of himself." The resurrection of Christ is the revelation of the recovery of man's "true self" as the "only creature on earth that God wanted for its own sake," that is, possessing a value—being someone, possessing a name—that cannot be evaluated in terms of anything else. Again, St. Paul: "For this reason (the sacrificial gift of himself on the cross), God exalted him to the highest place and gave him the name that is above every name" (Phil 2:9).

To summarize: The human vocation is most radically a call to existence out of nonexistence. It is the call to experience and live life as pure gift, as a gift of self, as sacrificial love. Christ is our vocation. His sacrificial love is the revelation of the human vocation. We cannot discover our true self except by making ours his sacrificial love, with all that this betokens. To live is Christ. A life inconsistent with Christ's sacrificial love operating within us is antihuman.

Now we are in a position to appreciate the tragic roots of our "crisis of vocation" and its many cultural manifestations.

# THE REFUSAL OF VOCATION

The myriad of negative cultural forces militating against an authentic experience and response to vocation are different manifestations of the rejection of Christ's sacrificial love. They are manifestations of sin, the refusal of the human vocation.

It is common today to speak of systemic evil, of sinful structures, even though sin, as such, is never found except in the free choice of a human person. "I will not serve" has seared itself into our human nature in such a way that Cain is forever killing Abel. The narcissistic fury expressed in Cain's words to God, "Am I my brother's keeper?" reveals the radical atomization of human relationships through sin, which renders covenant with God, which renders vocation, difficult, if not impossible. Not able to say he loves his brother whom he does see, Cain proclaims his inability to love God. In awful isolation, the individual cannot love himself and so there is only atrophy and death.

Together with the vocation to existence as pure gift, we experience in our culture many forms of another call: the call to nonexistence, the ideology of the serpent in the garden, the anti-Word, the antivocation, so to speak, the "signs and symptoms of death" as Pope John Paul II calls them in his latest encyclical, the "picture of death being composed in our age" (cf. DV, 57).

The drama of our time is what Cardinal De Lubac called the "drama of atheistic humanism." To put is simply: it is atheism provoked by fear of God, fear that living a life in which existence is accepted as pure gift and in which fulfillment found in self-giving to him in worship and love will lead to a loss of our freedom, our identity. Sacrificial love is feared as enslaving.

In fact, the very opposite, as we have seen, is the truth. That is why we can call this the anti-Word, the antivocation, the call to nonexistence. Deceived by that call, the human person refuses to accept others as gift, seeks to reduce others to instruments, to treat persons as things because the other is feared. God is feared in his image and likeness. Contraception; abortion; the unbridled pursuit of goods and success while trampling on the rights of those who cannot "contribute" or "produce"; the importance given to "having more" instead of "being more"; the arms race; the threat of nuclear destruction; the belief that unreserved, permanent commitments are useless and even impossible; torture and terrorism; the battle for power between men and women who consider their sexual differentiation—their bodies—as a mere accident of birth, if not a burden; the totalitarianism of politics; the triumph of materialism: all of these are more than cultural phenomena working against vocations.

They are the expression of the radical refusal of vocation called sin. They are experiences of an offense against God, of a rebellion against God, which is necessarily a rebellion against the other and the self. The revelation of the truth about the human vocation to personal fulfillment through sacrificial love, perceived in Christ crucified and risen, convicts this world of sin and exposes its need—not for growth, development, renewal, or whatever, but for redemption. Unless we see and call our present situation as it is in the light of the Gospel, we will be burying our faces in the ground and no amount of studies, meetings, and attractive programs to promote vocations will be worth anything. Our churches will continue to empty in judgment against us. Let us call our "vocation crisis" by its true name. It is the rejection of Christ as our vocation. It is once again his condemnation to death.

# THE BISHOP AND VOCATION

Our fundamental responsibility as bishops in this situation is to proclaim in an undiluted manner the reality of the redemption of the human vocation through that very death of Jesus to which sin condemns him. It is to proclaim forcefully the death of death, to proclaim the cross and resurrection as essential to the fulfillment of our human vocation to existence out of nonexistence. It is to tell the truth. Whether we are discussing the priesthood, religious life, marriage, the single life, or any vocation or ministry in the Church, we should be attentive to the underlying truth they all have in common: vocation to sacrificial love. The "crisis of vocation" is to be seen for what it is: a crisis of faith, a crisis of our call to holiness. This is not pessimism, but realism—the saving realism of the cross and resurrection of Christ.

In the epistle to the Colossians, St. Paul dealt with the tensions experienced by the apostle in the response to his vocation. He yearns for and prays that all might "attain full knowledge of [God's] will through perfect wisdom and spiritual insight" (Col 1:9).

What precisely is the insight that St. Paul hopes will resolve the tensions among the Colossians? It concerns the preeminence of Christ in creation, history, and the Church. This preeminence is the result not only of his identity as the "image of the invisible God" (Col 1:15), but also of his sacrificial death for us, "through the blood of the cross." Thus he has brought about reconciliation and unity. In order for this unity to be effective in us, it is necessary to "hold fast to faith, be firmly grounded and steadfast in it, unshaken in the hope promised you by the gospel" (Col 1:23) of which he, Paul, is the servant.

Paul experiences the sufferings of his apostolic life, endured for the disciples, as filling up "what is lacking in the sufferings of Christ for the sake of his Body, the Church" (Col 1:24). He sees the tensions and difficulties in his ministry from the perspective of what he calls "the mystery." This word for him designates the plan of God for the creation and redemption of the human person. The mystery sheds light on what is happening at any given moment in the history of the world and of God's people. What is happening—the Mystery—is nothing less than the process through which everyone is made "complete in Christ." This revelation of the mystery of man in the mystery of Christ, this anthropology derived from Christology: this is what sustains the apostle in his sufferings, confident of the Gospel's eventual triumph. So will it be for us a source of great confidence in spite of the current "crisis of vocation." There is no contradiction between the authentic development of persons and the demands of the Gospel. Rather, the former depends on the latter. That is why, in spite of his trials, St. Paul persists in his vocation to preach the mystery and to "admonish all men and teach them in the full measure of wisdom," intending, as he says, "to make every man complete in Christ. For this I work and struggle, impelled by that energy of His which is so powerful a force within me" (Col 1:28–29).

# MARY: VOCATION FULFILLED

We shall discover the path to follow and obtain the help we need by turning to the one in whom the human vocation revealed in the mystery of Christ finds its fulfillment: Mary, Mother of redeemed humanity, Mother of the Church.

The recent *Instruction on Christian Freedom and Liberation* states it thus: At the Lord's side, Mary "is the most perfect image of freedom and of the liberation of humanity and of the universe. It is to her as Mother and Model that the Church must look in order to understand in its completeness the meaning of her own mission" (97). Mary's assent is the Church's assent; it is redeemed humanity's assent to the human vocation. Her simultaneous virginity and motherhood reveal the Church's and redeemed humanity's total availability for fruitful sacrificial love. The universal vocation of the People of God will be fulfilled through her: "all ages to come shall call me blessed . . . his mercy is from age to age on those who fear him" (Lk 1:45–50).

For this, she has been set apart from the moment of conception. More radically than Jeremiah who was "dedicated" before he was born (cf. Jer 1:5), Mary is the one "full of grace," the "highly favored" one who is "blessed among women" (cf. Lk 1:28). Her assent takes the form of a bold proclamation: "I am the servant of the Lord" (Lk 1:38). This title does not indicate a passive acceptance of God's will; it betokens a mission to allow salvation history to be played out in and through her. It betokens a vocation, the vocation of God's people.

As sacrificial love, with heart pierced by the sword, her vocation required her to offer the fruit of her womb to and for others. This vocation reached its summit at the foot of the cross: "Woman, there is your son" (Jn 19:26). The Church was to discover in her the reality of the vocation of all redeemed humanity: "There is your mother" (Jn 19:27). As such, she was to be always at the side of the apostles (cf. Acts 1:14). In the letter to the Ephesians, St. Paul summarizes the vocation of the Church, of each one of her members, and indeed the vocation of humanity according to the creative and redemptive plan of God, as existing as the praise of God's glory (cf. Eph 1:12). This is the human vocation. This is Mary's identity: "My being proclaims the greatness of the Lord, my spirit finds joy in God my savior" (Lk 1:46–47).

Aided by Mary, still with us as she was with the apostles in the Upper Room, may we welcome the Spirit of courage and boldness, and offer to today's lonely, alienated humanity the liberating truth of Christ, our vocation; Christ in us, the hope of glory (cf. Col 1:27).

# VOCATION TO LAY LEADERSHIP IN THE CHURCH AND THE WORLD

## Raymond A. Lucker
## Bishop of New Ulm

One of the special signs of the presence of the Holy Spirit in the Church of modern times is the growth in the participation of the laity in the life and mission of the Church. The Holy Spirit is "moving lay [people] today to a deeper and deeper awareness of their responsibility and urging them on everywhere to the service of Christ and the Church" (AA, 1).

My personal experience with laity, lay organizations, and lay movements in the Church during the last forty years is probably typical. Many of us were seminarians and priests in the forties, fifties, and sixties and had a great deal of experience with various lay groups. And, there were many: Knights of Columbus, Holy Name Society, men's clubs, fraternal groups, Catholic Youth Organization, Altar and Rosary Societies, St. Vincent de Paul Society, the Catholic Central Union, Serra International, Labor Guilds, the Legion of Mary, Catholic Interracial Councils, Sodalities, Third Orders, and devotional groups. They touched all of our lives.

A distinguishing feature of all of them was that, for the most part, they were directed by the clergy. As a seminarian and young priest, I was thrilled by the encouragement given to the lay apostolate by Pope Pius XI and Pope Pius XII. I was excited about the specialized Catholic action movements and was involved with several of them: Young Christian Workers, Young Christian Students, the Christian Family Movement, and groups of doctors, lawyers, journalists, and business people. Pope Pius XI was called the "Pope of Catholic Action." He defined the lay apostolate as "the participation of the laity in the apostolate of the hierarchy." To be considered Catholic Action a group had to have a mandate from the bishop or another church authority. There was a great deal of discussion and controversy about the importance of the mandate and which groups could be officially considered Catholic Action. Gradually, there came to be a distinction between Catholic Action and the lay apostolate.

The way was being prepared by the Holy Spirit for a fuller treatment of the role of the laity in the Church and in society. The Second Vatican Council documents *Dogmatic Constitution on the Church, Pastoral Constitution on the Church in the Modern World, Constitution on the Sacred Liturgy,* and the *Decree on the Apostolate of the Laity* were preceded by the writings and addresses of Pope Pius XII, especially in his encyclical on the Mystical Body and in *Mediator Dei;* by theologians and writers like Congar, Suenens, Suhard, Cardinal Saliege, and others who continued to prepare the way; and by the experience and witness of lay people in many parts of the world.

I felt that the lay apostolate was an important part, indeed an essential part of the Church of the future. This was the direction in which the Church was going. "To restore all things in Christ" was the motto. During the summers when I was a seminarian in the 1940s, we participated in the summer schools of Catholic Action, organized and led by Fr. Daniel Lord, SJ. For a whole week, we attended short courses on different aspects of the lay apostolate and Catholic Action. I was a member of a group at the St. Paul Seminary that met every Sunday afternoon to discuss Catholic Action. We used pamphlets and books written by Msgr. Joseph Cardijn and others.

We got "the apostolic itch." A large group of us took a bus to Notre Dame during the summer of 1947 to participate in a conference for seminarians on Catholic Action. I remember driving to Chicago and Milwaukee with other seminarians, meeting with leaders of the Young Christian Workers and the Young Christian Students, with Catherine de Hueck Doherty at Friendship House. I recall coming into personal contact with the Catholic Worker. Father Keller came to speak to us about the Christophers.

I worked summers at the Catholic youth centers in St. Paul and Minneapolis, precisely so that I could participate in the excitement of the activity with committed young people working in apostolic endeavors. I came under the influence of marvelous priests like Fr. John A. Sweeney and Fr. Joseph Baglio. As a priest, I spent a couple of weeks each summer at Grailville in Loveland, Ohio, where young women shared community living, meaningful liturgies, and a growing awareness of the role of women in the Church. There was an experience of faith and prayer and international sharing.

I went to Ireland to meet with Frank Duff, the saintly founder and leader of the Legion of Mary. I stayed for several days at the international headquarters of the Grail in Holland, sharing with them their vision of the renewal of the Church. In Rome I met with Rosemarie Goldie, Australian Grail member, who was one of the first women to work in the Vatican at the International Council of the Laity.

My first assignment as a priest was to work with the Confraternity of Christian Doctrine in the Archdiocese of St. Paul, helping parishes call the laity to participate in the apostolate of religious education in various ways: teaching in the schools of religion; joining discussion groups and parent education groups; forming, with their pastors, parish boards for CCD; becoming involved in living-room dialogues and home visits; and helping in many ways to bring the gospel message to others. We read magazines edited by lay people: *Commonweal, Today, Work, Integrity.* In those days, the *Wanderer* was quite a forward-looking newspaper. It featured writers such as Fr. Virgil Michael, OSB, and Frederick P. Kenkel who promoted and encouraged the study of the social encyclicals of the Holy Fathers.

All of this is by way of reminder that the Second Vatican Council was not the beginning. But, Vatican II did make a giant step in a new direction.

## MISSION OF JESUS

We believe that the mission of the Church is the same as the mission of Jesus. Jesus was sent by the Father. He invites us. He calls us. He sends us. "As the Father sent me, so I also send you" (Jn 20:21).

The mission of Jesus, his very purpose for coming among us, can be expressed in a number of ways. Jesus came to show God's love for us. He came to redeem us, to save us. He came to share God's life with us. He called us to be his people, his body.

# KINGDOM

Another way to say it is that the mission of Jesus, his very purpose, was to inaugurate the kingdom of God. And the kingdom of God is wherever God's will is done, wherever God's will is at work. Jesus came to do God's will. He allowed the Father to reign in his heart and life completely. "He humbled himself, obediently accepting even death, death on a cross!" (Phil 2:8). He invites us to follow: "Take up your cross and come after me" (Lk 9:23). Doing the will of God, letting God reign over us—that is where the kingdom of God is.

The proclamation of the kingdom was at the heart and center of Jesus' teaching. He was sent to inaugurate God's kingdom among human beings. The Lord, by our free choice with the gift of God's grace, is to rule over our mind, our heart, and our actions. And, we are to work to bring his rule of truth and life, of holiness and grace, of justice, love, and peace to our society. These are the hallmarks of the kingdom of God.

The reign of God was begun in Jesus. At the very beginning of his public life he proclaimed, "The reign of God is at hand! Reform your lives and believe in the Gospel!" (Mk 1:15). The kingdom is spread when individual people accept Jesus as the Lord of their lives, as they seek to do God's will in everything, as they allow God to be present and at work in their lives. So the kingdom of God is within you. It grows as a mustard seed, as a yeast, when people in families, parishes, and communities love God above all things and love one another. Mary, the Mother of God, is such a perfect example of one who entered the kingdom. She did God's will in every way.

We, the followers of Jesus and the People of God, are to be a sign of God's kingdom already here and yet to come. We, the Church, are called to serve the kingdom and advance it among all people. The Church is at one and the same time the "saved" community and the "saving" community (*Lineamenta*, 14). The Church, which continues Christ's life and mission in the world, has no other purpose for its existence than to extend the kingdom of God to people of every nation, of every age, of every social and economic condition.

As I say, the kingdom is wherever God reigns, wherever God's will is done. The Lord, by the power of the Spirit and by our free choice, is to rule over our mind, our heart, and our actions. And, we are to work under the grace of God and the power of the Spirit to bring a rule of God's love, justice, peace, truth, fidelity, patience, and the rest to our society. "The kingdom of God is already in your midst" (Lk 17:21).

Jesus said, "I am the way, the truth, and the life" (Jn 14:6). By what he is and by what he says and does, he teaches us all *truth*. He shares his divine *life* with us, inviting us into union with him so that, as members of the family of God, we can call God our Father and our fellow Christians brothers and sisters. He calls us to follow his *way*, loving and serving God and one another.

*Sharing the Light of Faith: National Catechetical Directory for Catholics of the United States* puts it this way: "The Church continues the mission of Jesus prophet (truth), priest (life), and servant king (way). Its mission, like his, is essentially one—to bring about God's kingdom—celebrating the sacred mysteries and serving the people of the world. Corresponding to the three aspects of the Church's mission and existing to serve it are those ministries—the ministry of the Word, the ministry of worship, and the ministry of service. In saying this, however, it is important to bear in mind that the several elements of the Church's mission are inseparably linked in reality (each includes and implies the others), even though it is possible to study and discuss them separately" (NCD, 30). The Church is "a communion of life, of love, of truth" (LG, 9).

Pope John Paul II said once—I believe it was to young people in Yankee Stadium—"Jesus alone is the solution to all your problems. He alone is the Way, the Truth, the Life. He alone is the real salvation of the world. He alone is the hope of salvation." With all my heart I believe this.

## MINISTRIES

So Jesus invites us to continue his life and work. He gives gifts to use in ministries of word, of worship, and of spiritual life and service. "The laity, too, share in the priestly, prophetic, and royal office of Christ and therefore have their own role to play in the mission of the whole People of God in the Church and in the world" (AA, 2).

Over and over I have said to the people I serve: "All of us

are called by God to extend the kingdom of God. We are to be a community of praying, believing, worshiping, loving people. Jesus invites us to take an active part in his mission." And people have responded.

# VOCATION

It is important to consider here the meaning of vocation. Vocation is a call, vocation is an invitation. By our very baptism and confirmation every single member of the Church is called to share in the life and mission of the Church. There is no shortage in the call of the Spirit to extend the kingdom of God. Baptism is "the very root of the Christian vocation. . . . In Christ and in the Church there is no inequality arising from race, nationality, racial condition or sex, for 'There does not exist among you Jew or Greek, slave or freeman, male or female. All are one in Christ Jesus' (Gal 3:28)" (*Lineamenta*, 16).

A key teaching about the vocation of the laity is given in The Dogmatic Constitution on the Church. "The laity are gathered together in the People of God and make up the Body of Christ under one Head. Whoever they are, they are called upon, as living members, to expend all their energy for the growth of the Church and its continuous sanctification. . . . The lay apostolate, however, is a participation in the saving mission of the Church itself. Through their baptism and confirmation, all are commissioned to that apostolate by the Lord Himself. . . . The laity are called in a special way to make the Church present and operative in those places and circumstances where only through them can she become the salt of the earth. Thus every lay [person], by virtue of the very gifts bestowed upon him [or her], is at the same time a witness and a living instrument of the mission of the Church herself" (LG, 33). "Hence, there is no member who does not have a part in the mission of the whole Body" (PO, 2).

The gifts of the Spirit are many and varied. "Just as each of us has one body with many members, and not all the members have the same function, so too we, though many, are one body in Christ" (Rom 12:4–5). "In the Church there is diversity of ministry but unity of mission" (AA, 2).

What is the teaching of the Second Vatican Council about the vocation of the laity? It is that *all are called.* All are called to share in the life and mission of the Church. All are called by their baptism and confirmation. All are called by the Lord himself. All are called to holiness. All are called within the very web of their existence. All are called as instruments of God to "renew the face of the earth" (Ps 104:30).

It is the teaching of the Council that *all are gifted.* All are gifted by the Holy Spirit. All are gifted in different ways so that there is "one mission but many ministries." All are gifted to transform the world and build up the Church.

First, all members of the Church are called to share in the teaching function (office, task) of the Church, and this is broader than the teaching function of the hierarchy. All of us share in the task of better understanding the gospel message, and all share in the prophetic and teaching office of Jesus. Bishops must be in touch with the experience of the faithful. The hierarchical teaching office has a God-given role of protecting the Church from heresy. Nevertheless, every member of the Church has a role in not only learning but in teaching and sharing their faith with their children, with their neighbors, with people in their communities, and with those with whom they live and work and engage in leisure activities.

All the faithful contribute to the development of doctrine that is understanding and more deeply penetrating into the mysteries of faith. There is energy in the body of the faithful, the *sensus fidelium.* We, as bishops, need to learn how better to listen to the laity.

Second, all members of the Church share in the priestly function (office, task) of Jesus. All of us are called to personal holiness, and all of us are called to share and participate in the worship of God in the liturgy. So, likewise, we are called to be joined in the life of personal prayer and to share our prayer experiences in the intimacy and quiet of communities gathered in the Spirit. All members of the Church are called to be involved in the forming of believers into a community—a believing, worshiping, sharing community in the ongoing process of conversion. The Church is at one time the "saved" community and the "saving" community (*Lineamenta,* 14).

Third, all members of the Church are called to share in the servant function of Jesus (cf. Mt 25:35).

As I have said, there has been a wonderful and Spirit-guided growth of ministries in the Church. As church leaders, we have promoted this. The shortage of ordained and vowed ministries has been an occasion for this growth. But, it has not been the reason for enabling the people of the Church. They have that by right as baptized and confirmed.

Throughout the country, there has been a veritable explosion of people accepting the call and the challenge to exercise ministries of all kinds within the Church. We have seen a multitude of new ministries. We have encouraged people in teaching ministries, youth work, pastoral care, some liturgical ministries, spiritual direction, ministries of concern for the poor, the widowed, peace and justice, but all of this within the Church and under church leadership and control. I refer also to the marvelous contributions made to the life of the Church by the Cursillo movement, Marriage Encounter, the Charismatic Renewal, RENEW, the Focolare movement, *Communione e Liberatione,* and so forth.

Where we have not done so well is in recognizing, affirming, encouraging, and supporting people in ministries affecting the transformation of society, which is essentially *the* ministry of the laity and of all God's people. By "we," here I speak especially of bishops and church leaders.

Yet, the Second Vatican Council said, "The laity, by their very vocation, seek the kingdom of God by engaging in temporal affairs and by ordering them according to the plan of God. They live in the world, that is, in each and in all of the secular professions and occupations. They live in the ordinary circumstances of family and social life, from which the very web of their existence is woven. They are called there by God so that . . . they can work for the sanctification of the world from within, in the manner of leaven" (LG, 31). The laity comprise over 99 percent of the membership of the Church, and they have a rich and varied experience in every aspect of society.

Pope Paul VI put it forcefully in his Apostolic Exhortation *On Evangelization in the Modern World:* "Their [lay people's] primary and immediate task is not to establish and develop the ecclesial community—this is the specific role of the pastors—but to put to use every Christian and evangelical possibility latent but already present and active in the affairs of the world. Their own field of evangelizing activity is the vast and complicated world of politics, society and economics, but also the world of culture, of the sciences and the arts, of international life, of the mass media. It also includes other realities which are open to evangelization, such as human love, the family, the education of children and adolescents, professional work, suffering" (EN, 70).

Again, the *Decree on the Apostolate of the Laity* states: "Christ's redemptive work, while of itself directed toward the salvation of [all], involves also the renewal of the whole temporal order. Hence the mission of the Church is not only to bring to [people] the message and grace of Christ, but also to penetrate and perfect the temporal sphere with the spirit of the gospel. In fulfilling this mission of the Church, the laity, therefore, exercise their apostolate both in the Church and in the world, in both the spiritual and the temporal orders. These realms, although distinct, are so connected in the one plan of God that He Himself intends in Christ to appropriate the whole universe into a new creation, initially here on earth, fully on the last day. In both orders, the lay [person], being simultaneously a believer and a citizen, should be constantly led by the same Christian conscience" (AA, 5).

The Second Vatican Council stressed, first of all, the call of lay people to change the society in which they live and work; after that, they can be called to ecclesial ministries. "Besides this apostolate [to make the Church present and operative in those places and circumstances where only they can do it], which pertains to absolutely every Christian, the laity can also be called in various ways to a more direct form of cooperation in the apostolate of the hierarchy. This was the case with certain men and women who assisted Paul the Apostle in the gospel, laboring much in the Lord (cf. Phil 4:3; Rom 16:3ff.). Further, laymen have the capacity to be deputed by the hierarchy to exercise certain church functions for a spiritual purpose" (LG, 33).

We have reversed this order. We have tended to call people first to ministries within the church community and secondarily (or at least with far less emphasis) to ministries for the transformation of society. We need to make a distinction between ecclesial ministries and ministries in and for "the world." I believe that, while we have encouraged ministries within the Church, we have not clearly seen or supported ministries in the "world." I put quotation marks around the word *world* because the Church is in the world, too. Perhaps, it would be better to speak of ministries in the marketplace or engagement with the world of work, family, and leisure or ministry for the transformation of society.

It is especially in the family and society, in sexuality and economics, in marriage and in work that this transformation must take place. In our part of the country, we are going through a rural crisis of serious proportions. This crisis has helped me to understand a similar crisis—our attitude toward and our treatment of sexuality. Yes, every member of the Church is called to transform the world and that is particu-

31

larly needed in economics and sexuality in the world of work and in the family. In this, I laud the efforts made by Joe Holland, Wendell Barry, and Walter Brueggemann, to whom I am greatly indebted for what I say here.

There is a parallel in history between the way we (white males, especially) treat the land (and sea and sky) and the way we treat women. Land is looked upon as a commodity to be used, owned, exploited, dominated. Women were similarly considered. Land can be bought, sold, discarded. Land is an object of our greed, our covetousness. Women also. When women are degraded and exploited, sexuality is rejected as sacred, good, beautiful, powerful, to be treated with respect and responsibility. Human sexuality is degraded when it is trivialized, when people treat one another as sex objects, when there is little commitment.

Our land, our water, our air are being contaminated, used up, and polluted through greed and exploitation, contaminated by chemicals and nuclear fallout. Economic injustice results when a few can lay claim to absolute ownership of the goods of the earth. I see so many connections between pollution of soil, water, and land and sexual exploitation; between economic repression and preparations for war; between the rejection of God in the world of work and the rejection of God in human sexuality.

Yes, every member of the Church is called to transform the world. And, that is particularly needed in economics and sexuality; in the world of work and in the family. Marriage is a ministry. Work is a ministry.

Jesus is savior. He came to bring salvation to the whole world and to all things. What was "finished on the cross" was only the beginning of the transformation of the world and the transformation of society. The world is not transformed in church. The first and most important apostolic work of any parish, after the worship of God, is what people do in their homes as mothers and fathers, sisters and brothers, and in the incarnation of the Gospel in life through what people do at home and on the job, in the neighborhood or community, where people really live.

Everything that is done in a parish by way of religious education and participation in worship is to prepare people for bringing all things under the headship of Christ. The only way that Christ's kingdom will be established on earth is through lay Christians bringing under God's reign the reality of the world in the family, in social life, in business, and in the political world. Parishes will be strong when people feel and see the connection between faith and work, between Sunday morning liturgy and Monday morning work, between seeing God's presence at the altar and seeing him at the clinic, the desk, the farm, and the sink.

The laity's unique role is to make the Church present in society and to transform the political, economic, and social institutions in the light of the Gospel. "God's plan for the world is that [people] should work together to restore the temporal sphere of things and to develop it unceasingly. Many elements make up the temporal order: namely, the good things of life and the prosperity of the family, culture, economic affairs, the arts and professions, political institutions, international relations, and other matters of this kind. . . . All of these . . . possess their own intrinsic value. This value has been implanted in them by God. . . . It has pleased God to unite all things, both natural and supernatural, in Christ Jesus 'that in all things he may have the first place' (Col 1:18)" (AA, 7).

The Chicago Declaration of 1977 urged Church leadership to nurture and support laity in their role as Church in the world. It is important to the life and ministry of the Church to reclaim this vision.

## SOME PROPOSITIONS

I come now to a series of propositions, which I see as flowing from a theology of laity and the vocation and mission of laity in the Church and society.

1. It is essential for us bishops to listen to the laity. It is important in order to hear their real problems, pains, and joys. As I consulted with people in the preparation of this talk, no other issue was mentioned more often than this.

We listened to the laity in developing the *National Catechetical Directory.* We consulted with the laity in developing the pastoral letters *To Teach As Jesus Did, Called and Gifted,* and *The Challenge of Peace,* as well as in our dialogue in preparation for the pastoral letter on the economy. We have learned from experience of the importance of listening to the laity as we develop pastoral statements and plans.

All the faithful can contribute to planning and decision making in the Church. There are ways to tap into this. The diocesan pastoral council, parish councils, finance committees, and other parish and diocesan committees are important

vehicles for listening to the laity and for developing diocese-
san or parish goals. They need to be encouraged and taken
seriously. But, this is not enough. We need to listen on *their*
turf, in *their* living situations. We began to do this in the Call
to Action process during the bicentennial. We especially need
to listen to those who are marginalized, which is, after all,
where Jesus began his ministry. Somehow, we have to listen
to those who have left practice of their faith.

It is important to listen to the laity in questions of marriage, family, and sexuality. This seems to be so obvious since
theology is faith seeking understanding. That is, it is a reflection on experience in the light of faith.

It is important to listen to the laity, to hear their reflection
on the experience of living the message of the Gospel. This is
an important source for theological reflection. It is important
to listen to the laity to hear answers to the application of the
gospel teachings in social, political, and economic issues. "An
individual [person], by reason of the knowledge, competence,
or outstanding ability which he may enjoy, is permitted and
sometimes even obliged to express his opinion on things
which concern the good of the Church" (LG, 37). The bishop
plays a special role in promoting this listening process.

2. We need to support the laity in *their* ministry, namely in
their role as Church in the world of work, family, and leisure.
We need to help lay people see that in their everyday life, in
their families, in their work, and in their recreational activities they are the Church. We need to affirm them in the beautiful things they do in the care for their children, in their love
for one another, in their committed sexual expressions in
marriage, in their daily relationships in their neighborhood
and community. Let them go with it. We need to be careful of
clericalization of lay ministries and recognize that it is properly the ministry of the laity to be involved in political, social,
and economic life. They are involved in the apostolate of the
laity by right, not by our permission. There is a real issue of
power and control here.

3. There is need for a positive theology of sexuality. All of
us need to proclaim to the housetops the words of the Second
Vatican Council that say sexual intercourse in marriage is
good: "Hence the acts in marriage by which the intimate and
chaste union of the spouses takes place are noble and honor-
able" (GS, 49).

Men and women are created equal and in the likeness of
God. We are God-like in our very sexuality. More of us, and

especially more married people, need to speak of human sexuality, especially conjugal sexual relationships, as a precious gift of God—a joy, and the basis of life and love. Married people worship God in their sexual lovemaking.

As bishops, our first need in this regard is to accept and love our own sexuality and seek healing where we have been wounded and to grow as sexual human beings. We need to help free people to rejoice in their sexuality. We need to listen to married people and encourage them, support them in sharing their insights with others in small groups, with their children, and with couples preparing for marriage.

4. There is a need to continue to support lay people in ecclesial ministries. We need to continue to foster, encourage, and oversee the participation of the laity in ministries of Word, worship, and service. This is particularly true in supporting those people who wish to devote their lives to ecclesial ministries. I am firmly convinced that there is no shortage of vocations to ministries in the Church. There is, of course, a great shortage of vocations to the priesthood and to the traditional apostolic religious communities.

5. There is a need, however, to develop scholarship opportunities for people who have heard the call of serving the Church in professional lay ministry. Over a long period of time, we have provided scholarships for our seminarians. Every diocese has a burse fund, an endowment fund to provide tuition, room, and board to young men studying for the priesthood and to priests engaged in continuing education. We need to develop similar scholarships for people who are training for ecclesial ministries.

6. In addition to that, it is so important that we provide adequate salaries to support lay people and their families. This includes not only adequate salaries, but also and especially health insurance, a pension plan, and opportunities for continuing education.

7. Lay people receive much of their information about the Church and church teaching through the secular press, according to sociological studies made by Fr. Andrew Greeley and others. (This is not to deny the importance, yes, even the necessity of a strong Catholic press.) It is important for us to be open to the press and to use every opportunity that we can to provide it with information, statements, and church teaching. All our meetings and the meetings of the International Synod should be open to the press. We discovered from experience that the policy of secrecy at the Second Vatican Council

was not a good one, and the excitement of the Council grew as more people learned of its daily workings.

8. We need to do a much better job in instructing our people about the truths of faith, our traditions, and our heroes. There is a well-educated and independent population of Catholics who are not about to leave the Church, yet are woefully ignorant of their Catholic heritage. On one hand, some speak of truths of faith and morality in terms of "my opinion." On the other hand, some are becoming their own magisterium, throwing accusations of heresy and modernism at anyone who disagrees with them. Neither group recognizes the difference between faith and theology.

9. The role of women in the Church and in society is an especially critical one today. For right or wrong, we bishops are perceived as being inattentive to women's issues and concerns. We are perceived by some as enemies, as patriarchs, and even as being frightened of women. It seems to me especially important that we support women in their ministries and in true Christian feminism. We need to pursue this more vigorously. For example, we have not taken the leadership in changing exclusive language in the liturgy, in official documents, in hymns, and so on. We need to express our views more forcefully. We are perceived as being insensitive on this issue. Indeed, we have to face the fact that some of us *are* insensitive. I acknowledge that I am often part of the oppression that women feel. For this, I ask forgiveness.

10. There is a very helpful discussion being developed on the relationship between economy and sexuality, between work and the home, between our treatment of land and our treatment of women, which I think merits attention and discussion.

11. In my opinion, the most serious problem facing the Church is the need for conversion among adult Catholics. There is a need to recognize that we are an adult Church; that many Catholics are well instructed but not evangelized; that many Catholics are cultural Catholics, social Catholics, rather than committed, faith-filled, believing Catholics. We need to give higher priority to evangelization within the Church. We need to recognize that adult Catholics need evangelization, that they need to be continually converted. And that, of course, includes ourselves.

12. We need to see, therefore, the importance of witness. Faith is a gift of God that comes through the witness of others, especially the witness of the community. Our experience with

small faith-sharing groups tells us a great deal about the importance of witness, about the importance of sharing faith. There is a need for improved preaching, not necessarily exegetical preaching, but homilies that relate to the lives of the particular community addressed. Occasional preaching by a lay person may indeed be both motivating and necessary in this regard.

Programs for ongoing growth in faith ought to grow out of the felt and expressed needs of our people. The human experience of the people must count for something when we consider both short- and long-range programs or processes to strengthen, deepen, and renew the people's faith life.

13. Holiness is for all, which means that holiness includes life in the world of work, in sexual relationships in the family, and in our recreational activities. As we said in our pastoral letter *Called and Gifted:* "Lay men and women hear the call of holiness in the very web of their existence (LG, 31), in and through the events of the world, the pluralism of modern living, the complex decisions and conflicting values they must struggle with, the richness and fragility of sexual relationships, the delicate balance between activity and stillness, presence and privacy, love and loss" (p. 3).

Holiness is nourished by prayer, by listening to the Lord. Let me tell you about Lela. She is a friend, a widow in her seventies, living on social security. She has experienced great hardship, suffering, and grief in her life. Forty-five years ago, she and her husband, who were at that time going through a particularly stormy period in their marriage, came to know the importance of daily scripture reading, meditation, and sharing in their lives. Lela says, "God has a plan for us and we can know that plan." Almost every day for over forty-five years, she and her husband spent some quiet time each morning, twenty minutes or so, reading a scripture passage and then quietly, prayerfully listening. After their meditation, they jotted down their thoughts and then shared them with each other. They have become convinced that it was during these times that God guided them, spoke to them. No major decision or activity was begun without this "guidance."

Yes, lay people have a vocation. They are called to share in the mission of Jesus. They are gifted by their baptism and confirmation to be witnesses to the ends of the earth and, through the power of the Spirit, to renew the face of the earth.

# THE DESERT WILL BLOSSOM VOCATION STATISTICS, RESEARCH, AND ACTION PLANS

Lawrence H. Welsh
Bishop of Spokane

As bishops we are personally concerned with vocations, not only because the Second Vatican Council[1] and the new *Code of Canon Law*[2] have stated that we must show the greatest concern to promote vocations, but also because our personal pastoral sensitivity compels us to address this major concern of the Church.

Many of us personally bear witness to the words of our Holy Father when he said, "The problem of priestly vocations—and also of male and female religious—is, and I will say so openly, the fundamental problem of the Church."[3]

In the face of this challenging situation, however, we cannot afford to forget that we are men of faith. And, as men of faith, we "are also in a certain way in a season of a new advent, a season of expectation."[4] Guided by the Spirit, the Church is

---

1. *Christus Dominus*, 3, 15; *Optatam Totius*, 2.
2. *Revised Code of Canon Law* (1983), c. 233.
3. Opening Sermon at the International Congress for Ecclesial Vocations, Vatican City, May 10, 1981.
4. Pope John Paul II, *Redemptor Hominis*, 1.

sure that "the desert will blossom."[5] We "believe that Christ, who died and was raised up for all, can through his Spirit offer all the light and strength to measure up to his supreme vocation."[6]

A strong faith will see us through the present vocation crisis, regardless how much that faith is tested by doubt and tempted by despair. Our approach must be a generosity of heart and mind that enables us to read correctly the signs of the times and plan for a future not entirely of our making or under out control.

The expectation for any speaker is to provide answers and solutions. Let me tell you at the outset that I have no ready-made answers or easy solutions. As a fellow bishop, I share all your anxiety and personal concern for the future stability and leadership of our Church.

I have been asked to share with you some findings gleaned from current research on vocations, including statistics and survey data. In this light, I will highlight what we know about the sources of vocations to the priesthood, as well as the causes of the lack of vocations.

Time permitting, I shall present to you projects for fostering vocations, designed by two task forces: one on vocations in general and another on Hispanic priestly vocations and formation programs. And, in conclusion, I shall make four observations and five recommendations.

I do not intend to paint the barren desert to look like a verdant valley. I do hope, however, that we can gain a vision and a hope for the future that are built on the Spirit "who provides and directs the Church with various gifts, both hierarchical and charismatic, and adorns her with the fruit of His grace."[7]

# VOCATION RESEARCH STATISTICS

## Statistics

In 1984, the United States Catholic Conference (USCC) published a book entitled *Research on Men's Vocations to the Priesthood and the Religious Life*.[8] This volume summarized all available studies on men's vocations to the priesthood.

---

5. *Isaiah* 35:1.

6. *Gaudium et Spes*, 10.

7. *Lumen Gentium*, 4.

8. Dean R. Hoge et al., *Research on Men's Vocations to the Priesthood and the Religious Life* (Washington, D.C.: USCC Office of Publishing and Promotion Services, 1984).

Since then, a few more excellent studies have been published. These works provide the basis for my remarks and observations.

The concern about the theology of vocation and the theology of ordained priesthood is known to us all. For a significant number of people, the very word *vocations* has taken on a new and enlivening meaning as the People of God increasingly (and rightfully) recognize their baptismal right to participate in the ministry of the Church. The once clear lines drawn between ordained and nonordained blur in the meanwhile, and the Church seems to be without the familiar landmarks to guide us through the present crisis.

My interest is not to solve the theological and ecclesiological questions that confront the contemporary Church. We do well, however, to mark their importance and make at least the mental notation that the crisis in vocations is not merely a matter of justifying statistics or renewing numbers of vocations. A significant part of our challenge is indeed a cultural phenomenon whose genesis reaches from postponed career choices among the young to the war psychosis that paralyzes their sense of hope and purposefulness.

Needless to say, there is grave concern about the numbers of vocations and numbers of priests in the United States. In the thirty years between 1955 and 1985, the United States Catholic population increased by 19 million. In 1955, there were 48,000 priests; in 1975 there were 58,000 priests; and currently there are about 56,000 priests. Compare this with the priest-to-people ratio. In 1955, the ratio of Catholics to priests was one priest for every 700 Catholics; in 1975, it was one priest for every 800 Catholics; and today, it is one priest for every 900 Catholics.

Demographic studies clearly indicate that the Catholic population in the United States is on the increase. At the same time as we obviously know the number of priests is declining. Lest we get too alarmed by these statistics, however, let me state that North America enjoys the most favorable ratio of priests to Catholics of any continent. In Asia, the ratio today is one priest for every 2,400 Catholics; in Africa, it is one priest for every 17,000 Catholics. Latin America's general ratio is one priest for every 7,000 Catholics; in Europe, it is one priest for every 1,100 Catholics. The world ratio is one priest for every 2,000 Catholics.

We far exceed the norm, yet there is little comfort in the statistics when we personally know of the hardship wrought on our people by the increasing shortage of priests.

Along a similar vein, no one needs to remind us that our priests are aging. A cursory view of any of our priest gatherings is sufficient evidence. The statistics only confirm our pastoral impressions. In 1981, the median age for priests in the United States was 56 years.[9] By the year 2000, the largest group of diocesan priests (39% of the total) will be between 56 and 75 years old.[10]

The numbers of seminarians are equally bleak. In 1965, we were preparing 48,992 persons for priesthood. Today, we have 10,800 seminarians.[11] Statistics for other vowed or consecrated vocations are equally challenging. Vocations to the permanent diaconate are the only notable exception.

The reasons for the decline in numbers are as complex as they are many. And, not all of the reasons are bad and discouraging. At the same time, these comparative figures alert us to a deepening crisis that demands immediate attention.

## Profile of Seminarians

Besides the numbers, what else do surveys show us about our seminarians? I would like to share with you the following data from a major study recently published by the United States Catholic Conference.[12] The two most influential factors motivating men to consider a priestly vocation are (1) a sense of inner calling; and (2) the example of a priest. Vocation talks, literature, and advertising have virtually no effect. Seminarians who responded say that the qualities they need most are responsibility and apostolic zeal. They have identified prayerfulness and the ability to relate with people as the most important qualities in religious ministry. Fewer of the respondents have been educated in college seminaries, although college seminary alumni have a higher rate of perseverance in theology and are more certain about their commitment to the priesthood.

Another study compared a random sampling of seminarians with a similar group sampled in 1966. While many of its find-

9. National Conference of Catholic Bishops, *Catholic Church Personnel in the United States* (Washington, D.C.: NCCB, 1984), 7.

10. Ibid., 7.

11. Adrian Fuerst, OSB, *Catholic Church Personnel*, 13.; and *U.S. Catholic Institutions for the Training of Candidates for the Priesthood* (Washington, D.C.: CARA, 1985), vi.

12. Cf. Eugene Hemrick and Dean Hoge, *Seminarians in Theology: A National Survey* (Washington, D.C.: USCC Office of Publishing and Promotion Services, 1986).

ings confirm data I have already presented, the study supplies other interesting information. Encouragement by parents and by priests is very crucial in nurturing a priestly vocation. Moreover, today's seminarians are more decisive, more comfortable with superiors, more interpersonally adequate, and less dogmatic than their 1966 counterparts. They also demonstrate less admitted psychopathology and have higher morale. They are more conservative and see the primary task of the Church as encouraging the Christian life rather than reforming the world. Today's group judge celibacy a more meaningful expression of dedication than their predecessors, and fewer of them would consider marriage if it were permitted. Hispanic seminarians are on the increase, but it is important that they be nurtured in Spanish-speaking communities and be provided with opportunities to minister to their own people during the years of formation.

These data seem to me both to confirm many of our pastoral observations and to provide a basis for prudent planning for vocation awareness programs and the recruitment of seminary candidates.

## Studies on Attitudes of Young and Adult Catholics

There are three increasingly popular studies by Dr. Dean Hoge that deserve mention. The first reports on the attitudes of Catholic college students toward vocations and lay ministries[13] and supports the following conclusions: (1) Catholic college students are open to broadened participation in church leadership. They are not critical of the priesthood in its present form, but they are open to changes. (2) A large number of student leaders—larger than for many years—are seriously interested in vocations, and whopping numbers of students are seriously interested in lay ministry. The overall number of people interested in church work is very high. (3) The two principal factors discouraging vocations today are celibacy and the lack of encouragement of young people. (4) About one-half of the respondents favor the ordination of married men and women. The strongest objection to a priestly calling is celibacy. This study leaves us with two important impressions: a very high number of persons are interested in church vocations if they are encouraged; and there is a very high number of persons ready to be involved in lay ministry.

---

13. Dean Hoge, *Attitudes of Catholic College Students toward Vocations and Lay Ministries.* Unpublished.

Dr. Hoge's second study[14] concerns the attitudes of Catholics toward the priest shortage and parish life. It portrays in broad strokes the context out of which the Church will call its priests in the not-so-distant future. This study supports the following conclusions: (1) A majority of Americans have not yet been personally affected by the shortage of priests. (2) Given the option of whether it is more urgent to recruit many more priests or to restructure parish leadership to include more deacons, sisters, and lay persons, most Catholics—and a very high percentage of younger Catholics—choose the latter option. (3) The Catholic laity is not prepared to accept any substantial reduction in sacramental, priestly service; if there is a shortage of priests, many nonsacramental tasks that priests now perform should be reallocated to lay persons. (4) The views of Catholic women on these issues are very similar to men's views on the same issues. The two main impressions I gained from the study were the following: the opinion of many that, regardless of whether there is a priest shortage or not, the parish as we know it should be restructured; and, if a shortage of priests comes, the laity will always want certain services from priests but will tolerate priests dropping other duties.

The final study[15] examined the views of priests with regard to the current vocation situation. This study supports the following conclusions: (1) Recently ordained priests rate their seminary training much more favorably than did priests ordained in 1975 or before. (2) Age differences on institutional questions within the American priesthood are larger than sociologists find in almost any other institution today. (3) On questions regarding the nature of the priesthood today, middle-aged priests are most open to changes, the young and the old less so. (4) On theological attitudes, the fifteen-year change is a mild shift toward seeing faith as an encounter with God rather than assent to creeds, toward greater individual religious authority in moral decision making, and toward more ecumenical openness. (5) Work satisfaction for all priests increased from 1970 to 1985, with the greatest increase being among diocesan priests and older priests. (6) Overall priestly morale is higher in 1985 than it was in 1970, and the specific sources of satisfaction have changed somewhat. (7)

14. Dean Hoge, *Attitudes of Catholic Adults and College Students about the Priest Shortage and Parish Life.* Unpublished.

15. Dean Hoge et al., *Attitudes of American Priests in 1970 and 1985 on the Church and Priesthood.* Unpublished.

The biggest frustrations felt both in 1970 and 1985 are the way authority is exercised in the Church, loneliness, the difficulty in making a real impact upon people's lives today, and celibacy. (8) The proportion of priests offering active encouragement to young men considering the priesthood rose markedly from 1970 to 1985.

# RESPONSES TO THE VOCATION QUESTION

## What Is the Question?

Having reported on these various surveys, let me return to one of our original questions. Is there a vocation crisis? Is there a priest shortage? Perhaps, the question is: Is there a ministry shortage? Certainly, if our Catholic people expect the same services from the same proportion of priests, and if even optimistic projections for the year 2000 are realized, and if we do not take steps to restructure our parish life and the ministry of our priests, we will realize a severe shortage in very short order.

Is the Catholic Church in the United States experiencing a vocation *crisis* or a vocation *explosion?* If you regard the present situation as a scarcity, a crisis, a shortage, then you may want to spend time, funds, and energy trying to get more vocations to the seminary and convents. On the other hand, if you believe the high numbers in the seminaries and novitiates in the 1960s was an anomaly and that now the laity are being called to their rightful baptismal positions, you may see a vocation explosion happening today. The time, funds, and energy should be used, in part, to give them adequate theological and pastoral training.

## Some Options

Several of us have already realized a shortage of personnel in our respective dioceses. Some of us have made plans and taken steps to meet the shortage. Some of these methods include clustering parishes; amalgamating parishes; closing parishes; assigning one priest to several parishes; assigning laity to celebrate scripture/communion services; assigning laity as "pastoral administrators"; redistributing priests; reinstating former priests or deacons; asking senior priests to become associates or take small parish responsibilities; ordaining more permanent deacons.

Still others suggest finding alternative sources for more priests in other countries; among older persons; from among Episcopal priests who have converted to Catholicism.

To a great extent we are still in the experimental stages of these options. Some of them are meeting with success; others, perhaps, are far less successful than we anticipated. Yet, they are all creative approaches to deal with a vocation crisis that severely threatens the life of the Church, and act we must. Would it not be better, however, if our actions as bishops were *pro*-active instead of *re*-active?

## Causes of the Shortage

Vocation directors tell us many of the same things we hear regularly: Today, there are few responding to God's call, for any variety of reasons. Those most often listed are the materialism of our society; the lack of encouragement from parents; the difficulty of seeing celibacy in a positive light; the difficulty of making a lifelong commitment; the lack of a strong faith life; the many opportunities in lay ministry; the indecisiveness of youth. We all know this list so well—all too well. Where does it stop? More important, where do we *start?*

## New Ministries

If we simply continue to react to the vocation scarcity, we shall surely live in a desert by the year 2000, if not before. Many of us are trying to see other flowers bloom in the deserts before us, flowers that we judged before to be only weeds. Ideas like shared responsibility in ministry, collaborative ministry, and new lay ministries of multiple varieties are often blown up like sand against our sensitive ears.

We often find ourselves caught between two cacti plants: the pressing need to preserve the integrity of our priestly and eucharistic community on the one side, and the charismatic call for developing lay leadership on the other. And, we ask: What is the Spirit of God leading us to? How do we continue to serve God in our times?

# VOCATION PROMOTION/ AWARENESS PROGRAMS

During the past two years, two task forces were formed and coordinated by the NCCB Secretariats on Vocations and

Priestly Formation. One task force designed programs for fostering vocations to the priesthood and religious life; the other focused more specifically on Hispanic priestly vocations and formation programs.

## Called by Name

The first program is titled *Called by Name* and is a creative approach to vocation identification based on the methods used by the apostles to expand their numbers. In the early Church, if you will recall, the names of individuals were submitted to the community, and the Holy Spirit was called upon for guidance in making a selection, as we read in Acts 6:1–7.

Further, one of the most constant themes to appear in patristic literature with regard to ministry is "that of the candidate's hesitation or even refusal to take an ecclesiastical office upon himself, primarily out of a sense of unworthiness. Among those stricken with such hesitancy were some of the most illustrious of the Fathers."[16] Those who hesitated when "called by name" include Ambrose, Gregory Nazianzen, Augustine, John Chrysostom, and Ammonius. Naming, and even forcing, a person into ministry has ancient roots.

In our program, *Called by Name,* the faithful will be challenged to appreciate and accept the vocation God has given them to live, whatever that call might be. Further, individuals will be challenged at information retreats to consider the variety of ministries and services that exist in our Church today. In particular, men and women will be personally "called by name" and asked to consider serving the Church as priest, brother, or sister. Members of our parishes will be asked to recommend names of individuals in the 18 to 35 age group who they believe have the qualities for a vocation to the priesthood or religious life and who may be called by the Lord to these vocations. *Called by Name* provides the encouragement; the choice is up to the individual; the final selection is by the responsible bishop or religious superior.

Complete details of the programs have been outlined and clearly presented in a booklet. All needed materials and procedures are available. Any vocation office can readily adapt its many resources and activities to derive major benefit from this program. It has been pilot-tested in several dioceses and

---

16. Boniface Ramsey, *Beginning to Read the Fathers* (New York: Paulist Press, 1985), 119–121.

has proved to be very beneficial, not only for promoting vocations, but also in bringing greater awareness to a parish regarding its responsibility in promoting and forming vocations.

## Hispanic Vocations and Priestly Formation

Let me move to the proposals designed by the second task force—the one concerned specifically with Hispanic priestly vocations and formation programs. I probably do not need to illustrate the opportunity presented to the Catholic Church in the United States by the Hispanic presence. However, let me cite one fact to illustrate this opportunity. During a period of fifty years in the 1800s, approximately 2.2 million Irish and German Catholics arrived in the United States, usually with Irish and German priests who spoke their language. By comparison, in only a ten-year period between 1970 and 1980 over 5 million Spanish-speaking Catholics have entered and remained in the United States, usually not accompanied by Spanish-speaking priests.

The NCCB-sponsored task force responded to this need, and its proposals are now being implemented. The program consists of three categories: (1) vocation awareness; (2) vocation recruitment; and (3) priestly formation.

The first category concerns vocation awareness. Since Hispanics historically have observed that their priests were supplied from a "foreign" source, our action plan calls for two tactics (1) develop an orientation program to train local lay vocation recruiters, and (2) make every effort to place Hispanic vocation awareness on the agenda of lay Hispanic organizations.

The second category, also with two action plans, concerns vocation recruitment. Since recruiting from the Hispanic community requires appropriate insights and skills, these two elements are directed toward expanding the number of Hispanic and Hispanic-conscious vocation personnel. First, as chairman of the Bishops' Committee on Vocations, I suggest for your consideration the appointment of a Hispanic or Hispanic-conscious vocation director for your diocese. Second, in January 1987, at St. Thomas Villanova University in Miami, there will be a special orientation program to train vocation directors specifically for recruiting Hispanic vocations.

The third category, priestly formation, contains eight action plans that clarify needs specific to the Hispanic population and seek to provide those resources that are necessary for young men to pursue the priesthood.

We approved these plans at our November 1985 General Meeting in Washington, D.C. They are in the process of being implemented by our NCCB Secretariats on Vocations and Priestly Formation, in collaboration with other appropriate NCCB units. Your prayerful and personal support will assist greatly their effective implementation.

# CONCLUSION

In this presentation, I have tried to give an overview of the present vocation situation in the United States. We have looked at vocation statistics, and you have heard the results of the most recent research on vocations and seminarians. You have heard what current and future campus ministry leaders and students envision for the Church. I have shared with you the suggestions some persons are offering to head off any severe crisis resulting from the inevitable priest shortage. Further, I have shared with you the two plans designed by the special vocation task forces, which are now being implemented through our NCCB offices.

As I mentioned in the beginning of this presentation, I cannot change into a verdant valley what may very well become a desert. I do believe, however, that the Spirit of God is over our land and is trying to tell us as leaders to read the signs of the times. The desert will blossom again, not necessarily with the more recognizable single flowers we have known in the past, but with a harvest of new vegetation that may indeed dazzle our eyes.

In conclusion, I would like to make four observations and five recommendations. First, the observations.

1. Simultaneous with some disappointing reports, there are positive findings. On one side, we hear of decreasing numbers of seminarians; decreasing numbers of clergy; an ever-increasing average age of clergy; and reports of inappropriate clerical behavior. At the same time we hear that clergy morale is higher today than it has been in twenty years; the proportion of priests offering active encouragement to young men considering priesthood rose remarkably from 1970 to 1985; the quality of seminarians is higher than twenty years ago; over 13 percent of college campus male leaders have recently expressed an interest in vocations for themselves; in 1985,

priests rated their seminary training more favorably than did the priests in 1970; and work satisfaction increased for all priests from 1970 to 1985. Since priests are key to vocation encouragement and recruitment, the positive seems to be outweighing the disappointing.

2. We know the character of our eucharistic Church would be altered without sufficient priests. In fact, as bishops, we hold and teach sincerely that the Christian community cannot fulfill its complete mission without the ministerial priesthood. However, at the same time, we must recognize the sign of the Spirit in the great number of laity participating fully, actively, and intelligently in the life of the Church. Moreover, we can rejoice at the increasing lay enrollment in theology classes. Research establishes that, given the option, most Catholics think it more urgent to restructure parish leadership than to recruit many more priests. Pope John Paul II appears to support further investigation of this concept.

3. In light of the urgings of *Christus Dominus*, it appears responsible for this episcopal leadership to strike a balance between the legislated discipline of the Church on the one hand, and on the other, the findings of religious research we have sponsored, the observations of many vocations personnel, and the requests of other episcopal conferences.

4. The fourth and final observation is obvious and pastoral. While the ratio of priests to Catholics is decreasing, the ratios are already much more severe in the Hispanic, black, Asian, and native American populations. As pastors of all the people, our hearts must be concerned about this situation.

These four observations only skim the surface of the many responses possible to the wealth of data collected in so many recent studies. Your pastoral sensitivity to these concerns will undoubtedly generate many others.

I wish to add five recommendations to these observations.

1. Recognizing the severity of the priest shortage that confronts us, I encourage each of us to identify vocations to the priesthood as one of our administrative priorities in our respective dioceses.

2. Second, as a follow-up to the previous recommendation, while there are many formats for making vocations an administrative priority, consideration may be given to successful programs in other dioceses. For example, Bishop Delaney of Fort Worth brought together the entire presbytery for two full days in order to make the priesthood more attractive to themselves and to discuss specific ways to increase the number of semi-

narians in the diocese. Such days can be very worthwhile experiences.

3. A few dioceses have put together complete vocation promotion programs. Mention was made earlier of the program *Called by Name.* Some consideration may be given to supporting and implementing one of these specific programs in your diocese. As you know, in his message this year for the World Day of Prayer for Vocations, Pope John Paul II stressed the role of the pastor and the parish in promoting vocations. This year would be a timely occasion to have each parish initiate its personal vocation promotion program.

4. To clarify and articulate the theology of vocation to priesthood, I suggest that this body request our Holy Father to consider "The Divine Call: The Situation of Priestly Vocation" as the topic of the next World Synod of Bishops after the 1987 Synod on the laity.

5. The fifth and last recommendation is to remain strong in resisting the temptation to lower the standards in accepting candidates. Reports are received periodically that candidates rejected by one diocese or religious community have been accepted by another diocese or community without any reference to the candidate's former application. While no church law requires any consultation or release, prudent protocol and the good of the Church would suggest informed consultation.

The very subject of vocations that gathers us together is sufficient indication that we are in a state of crisis. We need not hide from the facts nor turn our face away from the trends, which our society speaks so persistently to us. God works in and through our world. With faith we will find our way—even if that way leads us for a while through a seeming desert. God, the giver of all vocations, stands at our side and will give us the wisdom if we but listen. Faith tells us that the desert before us will blossom indeed—with time, prayer, and perseverance.

## SELECTED BIBLIOGRAPHY

Butler, Frank, ed. *Laborers for the Vineyard: Proceedings of a Conference on Church Vocations.* Washington, D.C.: USCC Office of Publishing and Promotion Services, 1984.

Hemrick, Eugene and Hoge, Dean R. *Seminarians in Theology: A National Profile.* Washington, D.C.: USCC Office of Publishing and Promotion Services, 1986.

Hoge, Dean R. *Attitudes of Catholic Adults and College Students about the Priest Shortage and Parish Life.* Unpublished.

_____. *Attitudes of Catholic College Students toward Vocations and Lay Ministry.* Unpublished.

Hoge, Dean R.; Potvin, Raymond H.; and Ferry, Kathleen, M. *Research on Men's Vocations to the Priesthood and the Religious Life.* Washington, D.C.: USCC Office of Publishing and Promotion Services, 1984.

Potvin, Raymond, H. *Seminarians of the Eighties: A National Survey.* Washington, D.C.: National Catholic Educational Association, 1986. Unpublished.

The Vatican. *The Conclusive Document: Developments of Pastoral Care for Vocations in the Local Churches, Experience of the Past and Programs for the Future.* Vatican City: May 1982.

# VOCATIONS TO
# RELIGIOUS LIFE IN THE CHURCH

## Joseph A. Francis, SVD
## Auxiliary Bishop of Newark

How do I begin? Where do I begin? I come from an ethnic group that has maintained its tradition and history for thousands of years, through difficult times and in tragic circumstances, by using the art of storytelling. So, I am going to tell my story and bits and pieces of other people's stories—the stories of men and women who became religious.

In the past three years, there has been a flurry of activity by the Holy See and local dioceses relative to arriving at better communication with religious communities. We have heard, read, and learned many new things about religious life. There is ample evidence to show that attitudes are changing—both on the part of bishops and religious. From a long historical perspective, we have been exposed to the histories of religious communities—some heroic and inspiring, some scandalous and disintegrating, some quiet yet terribly effective in the history of the Church and society. From the twelfth century until now, the Church has canonized many religious. Our experience with religious has caused us to draw many conclusions about religious life. Some of us have oversimplified, stereotyped perceptions of religious life in general and, perhaps, of some groups of religious in particular. And, because we are bishops, teachers, movers and shakers, we have great impact and influence on just how Catholics and others view religious life. Many vocations to the religious life will live or die based on how we may view religious life and articulate our beliefs. In this paper, I shall attempt to speak candidly about religious and the vocation to religious life from a very positive experiential point of view, limiting myself to what we know as active religious life.

## THE CALL

For me, religious life was not a call to Camelot. I was totally unaware of the theology of religious life, the history, the demands, the charisms, and the scope of the ministry of the religious community to which I, as a determined twelve-year-old, applied. I knew this much, however: I had been told when I was about nine years old that I could never become a priest because I was colored. Now, some fifty years later, it all comes back to me.

I joined the Society of the Divine Word in 1936 because it was the only order I knew that took colored young men to become priests and brothers. I did not know in 1936 what I later discovered, namely, that my acceptance as a candidate was part of the theology of that order, that it was part of its missionary charism and spirituality, that it was part of its ministry. As simple as it may sound, my vocation and the vocation of hundreds of other black youth came to us because the Society of the Divine Word responded to the call of a God whose penchant for attracting and being attracted to the poor, the outcasts, the disenfranchised, and the victims of injustice was very much a part of the reason why the Society was established in the first place.

This Society would prepare over one hundred black young men for life as religious priests and brothers. Today, six of them are bishops. Over twenty of these young black religious became missionaries in Africa, Asia, Latin America, Polynesia, and the United States—north, south, east and west. I cannot deny that often I have been nagged by the knowledge that sometimes I wanted the opportunity to be a member of some other religious community—or some diocese. This was not possible in 1936. As paradoxical as it appeared then and now, my call came about because of the negative influences of segregation and racism in our nation and in our Church. I was called by God to an order that gave compelling witness to a commitment of positive action on behalf of racial and social justice. Along with the Josephites, the Society of the Divine Word is responsible for what *The Wanderer* describes as the "Gang of Ten" in the bishops' conference today. Seven of the ten are religious, belonging to four religious communities.

My story is not unique. Many of you, both religious and secular bishops, can recount stories of your own call in similar terms and under somewhat similar circumstances. There was nothing glamorous about our call, but we shall never be able to fathom the mystery of God's love and concern for us by which he has guided and formed us to be his witnesses, his ministers, and his servants to a needy world. Perhaps, if we are willing and able to understand this, we may see that the vocation to the religious life has a simplicity about it so profound that the very simplicity confounds us. The danger, however, is that we may attempt to view the religious vocation in a manner that is self-serving and even prejudicial to religious life itself.

## BISHOPS AND RELIGIOUS

As a religious and a bishop who is a religious in a conference of bishops made up of almost 95 percent nonreligious, I am often saddened and even hurt by what I perceive as a lack of knowledge and understanding, appreciation, and affirmation of many men and women in religious life. I am puzzled by the fact that, while so many of us have made giant strides in our understanding and implementation of Vatican II, we have maintained our stereotypes of religious in general. We have even complicated our relationships with religious as we seek to interpret and legislate for them, often without the benefit of knowing and understanding the intensive and painful processes through which most religious have come in the past twenty years. As bishops, we have renewed our dioceses, modified our life styles, downplayed our triumphalism, sought to emphasize collegiality and implement effective subsidiarity. We have done so at the cost of mistakes, some successes, a lot of pain, and confusion. Still, we have had our days of delight and joy. Yet, we have often been less than supportive of religious who have trodden the same paths we have walked with the same pain and ecstasy, the same successes and failures, the same hopes and fears, the same convictions and doubts. Lest I seem to lay too heavy a burden on bishops, I am convinced that much of this has happened because there was little or no communication, and both religious and the hierarchy have need for the truth about one another, which brings with it confidence; an atmosphere of mutual trust and respect; and, most of all, the realization that we are integral and vital members of the Church—the kingdom!

# THEN 1940

For a better understanding of the religious vocation, I shall take you on a short journey into the past—the recent past. When I entered the novitiate of the Society of the Divine Word in September 1941, I, like so many of you, belonged to an institutional Church that prided itself with having very clearly defined lines of authority. The rules and regulations by which we lived were strictly standardized. And, the order of the day was absolute conformity to the norms and mode of life from a past that had molded Catholics around the world for centuries. To be Catholic was to be identified clearly with a universe of uniformity.

Religious were even more conformed. The rules and regulations by which we lived were truly military in detail and enforced with a vengeance. The daily order, beginning at 5:15 A.M and ending at 9:00 P.M., was sacred and allowed for few, if any, deviations. We lived by a series of bells from the moment we awoke to the time the lights went out in the evening. We even had chimes that rang from the tower every fifteen minutes from 8:30 A.M. to 8:30 P.M., and at the sound of the chimes we paused to recite what was known as our quarterly hour prayers. Only outdoor recreation, meals, times of liturgy, and devotions were exempted. We examined our conscience twice a day, and each novice was provided with a small notebook to record transgressions. (I don't recall that I ever recorded any progress. I was too busy luxuriating in self-depreciation.) There were also sessions of public self-accusations and sessions in which selected novices accused others in public of real or perceived transgressions of the rules of conformity. Physical self-discipline, in imitation of the saints, was mandated at least four times a week.

Our conduct was as predictable as the changes in time and in seasons, but, happily, our ultimate orientation was toward our apostolates. These were clearly defined and canonized in our rule. There is no denying that those of us who survived were happy and good religious. What we went through was a small price to pay for the blessed happiness of making it to final vows and to the priesthood.

In the Church of the pre-Vatican II era, religious life, like the life of the institutional Church, was filled with symbolism. The whole symbolic world was so important to the Church and to religious life, and, if we have lost anything at all, we have discarded symbols of a rich past without fully finding new symbols or new meanings for old symbols. Some of the symbols were cassocks, habits, tonsures, heavy rosaries and crucifixes around our waists or necks, rings, scapulars, and so on. In my own order, the inside of the large waistband cincture was blood red to remind professed members of our special devotion to the Holy Spirit. It also served as a reminder that, as missionaries, we should be ever ready and willing to shed our blood. So consistent was our use of symbols and our understanding of those symbols in pre-Vatican II religious life that the youngest novice was able to appreciate the perfection of the manner in which the real symbol bearers—the older and even oldest members of the community—wore and demonstrated these symbols. You knew who the good and holy members were by the manner in which they evidenced in word and deed the symbols of the community. Even when a visiting member came from China, Latin America, India, or Germany and spoke no English, there was great comfort and solidarity as soon as the member and the community discovered how well the symbolic life of each conformed to the expected and the predictable.

Perhaps, the most difficult and damaging aspect of the institutional religious life, often experienced by many, was the dichotomy between what we were taught to expect as we advanced in wisdom and knowledge and what we actually experienced in our heart of hearts. For example, we were taught from day one that "no one who puts his hand to the plow and looks back is worthy of the kingdom"; and that we must let "the dead bury their dead." In other words, the separation from family and friends was absolute and complete. Poverty placed one outside of dependence on family, and, conversely, family could expect nothing from the vowed religious.

Chastity moderated friendships and all forms of affection. St. Aloysius, who dared not even look upon the femininity of his own mother, was proposed as a fitting model for those seeking to grow in virtue. For those seeking to control and negate the urges and the needs they had for affection, friendships, and personal sharings, the best description I can conjure up to describe such a state of life is that we were the receptors of a glorious past, with no obligation to contribute to the present and future with creative, personal efforts.

The reality, however, was different. Each of us longed for the day we would be free enough to enjoy one another, sing songs of our own making, shape images that sought to enflesh the intangible, linger to enjoy a sunset without feeling guilty, and to feel good about the world and people around us without becoming outcasts. And, because the reality differed from the model of institutional religious life, we adjusted to reality.

The era I have just described produced a plethora of great men and women. They were talented, generous, inventive, and holy. It was through their insights and the manner in which they were able to modify and qualify the model of Church and religious life in which they were formed that they could lead, support, and empower their communities to welcome and acclaim Vatican II as so necessary, so refreshing, and so challenging. I believe we have to remind ourselves that, although half of us in the room are post-Vatican II bishops, we are all pre-Vatican II Catholics who in some degree had to be conditioned by an Advent-like preparation for the coming of the Second Vatican Council. There were surely among us prophets—John the Baptists and curious men and women who tried to follow Jesus in order to discover where he lived.

## WHAT ARE MANY RELIGIOUS STRIVING FOR TODAY?

In the first part of this paper, I mentioned that for a period of time the Church, in many ways, and men and women religious had given up many symbols and had modified their life styles in an atmosphere of great difficulty. There was internal dissension, breaking up of some communities to form splinter groups, defections, and alienation between religious communities, with persons on both sides assuming "holier than thou" attitudes.

While this period ushered in a moment for the initiation of renewal aimed at the twenty-first century, sadly enough, it also became a time for regression. For some, it encouraged progress, for others, a frustrating sense of loss. For some, it was the beginning of orderly, prayerful change; for others, the beginning of chaos bordering on anarchy and revolution. Men and women religious in the United States experienced all the conditions I have just described. However, the most painful condition was the alienation that took place within religious communities and among religious communities of women and some members of the hierarchy, the clergy, and laity.

But, out of all of this, we are beginning to see some very positive results. New symbols are slowly emerging. Some may see them as a reaffirmation of old symbols and others as new symbols that speak a new language. Many men and women religious have progressed from the kinds of introspective preoccupations demanded by internal renewal to looking beyond the restrictive worlds of their own communities. They have, like many of their founders, viewed themselves as people of the kingdom—as gospel people. They are sincerely seeking to answer today's questioning society with the words by which Christ identified himself to the disciples of John: "Go tell John what you have seen and heard. . . ."

The full text of that encounter is this: "John the Baptist has sent us to you with this message, 'Are you the one who was to come, or are we to look for someone else?'" At that very time, Jesus was healing many people of their diseases and ailments and evil spirits, and he restored sight to many who were blind. Then, he answered them: "Go and tell John what you have seen and heard. The blind are recovering their sight, cripples are walking again, lepers are healed, the deaf hear, the dead are brought to life again, and the good news is given to those in need. And, happy is the person who loses his faith in me" (Lk 7:18–23).

Today, as I speak to you, men and women religious all over this country are into a whole new mode and are quietly but effectively bringing new life and new visions, forging new symbols for their communities and for the Church with other religious communities and with the laity and clergy. This is done according to the following principles: (1) the following of Christ; (2) a loyal recognition and safekeeping of each community's special character and purpose (its charism); (3) participation in the life of the Church; (4) an awareness of the contemporary human condition and the needs of the Church; (5) an internal renewal of the spirit.

Religious communities of men and women are interpreting and implementing these principles within the wide spectrum of pluralism and pluraformity that exists not only between religious communities but within religious communities in which ethnic, cultural, and racial groups abound. My own order, which is relatively young and small, has representation from over thirty-three countries and is ministering in some forty countries. Communities such as the Jesuits, Dominicans, and Franciscans must have double and triple that kind of representation.

If one wants to have a handy measurement of where religious orders are today and what their experience is, I can assure you that my personal experience is that most of them, with few exceptions, including contemplatives, have responded to Vatican II by committing themselves to labor for the implementation of Vatican II's direction. They want to see to it that the Word, the Gospel, continues to be enfleshed. They want to be the servants of God's people in and out of the Church; to exercise a preference for the poor, the frustrated, the lonely, and the materially and spiritually hungry of our country and of the world.

I believe that the vast majority of men and women religious want to make it unmistakably clear that their response, their commitment, their service are motivated by a choice, freely made out of love and not fear. Even some of the most conservative (I use this term in a nonpejorative sense) orders of men and women would be hard pressed to push their religious communities back into a concentration on the accidentals of religious life and not on its essentials. I cannot ignore the fact, however, that there are some in the Church at-large in this country and abroad who are presently attempting to do just that.

## MISSION VERSUS MAINTENANCE

When I arrived in the Archdiocese of Newark, I heard my own archbishop say frequently and forcefully that what he wanted to see most of all in his ministerial collaborators was a commitment to minister creatively. He did not want caretakers who saw their mission as one of maintenance only. When we pray for the coming of the kingdom, we certainly should do so conscious of the part each one of us plays in the progress that this kingdom makes, yet, fully aware that its fulfillment is for an undetermined future. To work for the kingdom to come is to continue to incarnate in our lives and activities the healing, forgiving, teaching, serving Jesus. To simply maintain what *is* demonstrates that we believe that the kingdom of God has already arrived and all we need do is to live in some sort of spiritually animated suspension.

In their efforts to renew themselves, religious communities refuse to view their mission as one of maintenance. They are looking at their apostolates, their constituencies, their rules, and they are making adjustments. They look at contemporary society and decide what they need. If necessary, they are willing to opt out of relationships and systems, especially economic systems, that belie their commitments to fidelity, celibacy, and simple living. When I speak negatively of maintenance versus creative mission activity, I am not suggesting that religious have abandoned their responsibilities to provide security for their sick and elderly or that the orderly recruitment, education, and formation of new members lose their places in the list of priorities. All of these, however, must be done for the sake of the kingdom of God on earth.

Many religious acknowledge that material goods bestowed upon them are not meant for the accumulation of wealth but for the prudent exercise of stewardship. There is a perception out there somewhere that some religious communities and dioceses have too much of this world's goods and that more effort is being spent on accumulating more and more to do relatively less for the building of the kingdom.

## THE AUTONOMY OF RELIGIOUS

While in the past religious clung desperately to their autonomy, today they are seeking to use autonomy to serve the Church in more creative and prophetic ways. This is no different from what Francis of Assisi, Ignatius Loyola, Don Bosco, Frances Cabrini, Mother Seton, Mother Mary Elizabeth Lange of the Oblate Sisters of Providence, Sister Mary Theodore of the Handmaids of Mary, and Josephine Aliquot, Henrietta DeLisle, and Juliet Gaudin of the Sisters of the Holy Family attempted to do. (The last five women founded communities of black sisters in New York, Baltimore, and New Orleans, respectively.)

Today, religious do not want to experience more dependence on the hierarchy. They desire to have themselves seen and appreciated as committed collaborators with the Church. They would prefer that their relationship to the Church in the United States and the leadership of that Church be celebrated in positive mutual respect and cooperation. They want old wounds bound up for healing so that new energies may be expended for the kingdom.

One need only have limited and infrequent views into many of our religious communities to realize and, hopefully, appreciate the fact that contemporary men and women religious are very conscious of the state of our nation. They see clearly that society is sharply divided between the relatively few who sit at Lazarus' table and those who sit and wait for the crumbs that may fall from that table. Materialism is all around us. Consumerism shrouds us like the foul smog that blankets our major centers of business and commerce. The symbols of such a society are possessions far beyond need and comfort—constant activity in search of pleasure and leisure with no commensurate effort; wastefulness in the face of want; and arrogance that shuns responsibility and compassion. The symbol of our nation, incarnated in our leaders, is military might of weaponry and sophisticated systems that will never be utilized and that become obsolete before they are off the assembly line. Surely, there is so much that is good in our country, but consumerism, militarism, and pleasure seeking for pleasure's sake militate against the basic human rights of individuals and groups and against the gospel values that seek to promote reconciliation, peace, compassion, and the freedom that flows from these virtues.

If religious can incarnate and exhibit the new symbolisms needed for our times, all of us will be richer. But the hierarchy, the clergy, and the laity must give approbation to religious and support and affirm those sincerely seeking to be a part of the Church's prophetic witnessing community. Too often, we have canonized such persons and such efforts only after a long delay, when we were not personally confronted and made uncomfortable by activities that challenged our complacency and maintenance posture in the building up of the kingdom.

Post-Vatican II religious are trying to show themselves and us that conformity is not the key element in their lives. Rather, it is accountability in building up the kingdom. It is accountability to the institution and the charism of their communities. It is respect for and accountability to the persons whom they serve and with whom they minister. It is accountability to the Church and loyalty to the leaders of that Church. Perhaps more than most in the Church, religious are eminently aware of and qualified to respond to the cultural, ethnic, and racial minorities and emerging pluralities in our nation today. These are reflected in the membership of many religious communities and most especially in their apostolates here in our country and all over the world. Hence, intercommunity and transcultural collaboration are very much a part of the ongoing activities of many religious communities.

Father Gray, SJ, whom I have paraphrased in so much of this paper, spells out the challenges facing religious and consequently facing us as members of the hierarchy. As we view vocations to religious life, we cannot be ignorant of the challenges faced by religious men and women today. They include the following:

- To create religious life styles and communities recognized as countercultural in their simplicity, hospitality, reconciling power, and humane asceticism. In short, to create new symbols for religious life in the 1990s and the twenty-first century.
- To create a structure throughout our initial and continuing formation where members are oriented toward accountability to the values of the kingdom.
- To create a discerning community that moves from accountability to a new level of synthesis (i.e., of recognizing new apostolic possibilities and needs from our mutual communication). This involves risks.
- To create a collaborative model of apostolic service where we trim away duplications, encourage joint projects, and enter into partnership for the kingdom.

I am sure that we are all painfully aware of the vast difference between our relationship to women religious and our relationship to men religious. Many men religious themselves, like the People of God in general, have yet to come to grips with the need for additional adjustments toward women in general and women religious in particular. Failure to do so is clear indication that we are either unaware of our own pre-Vatican II myopia or that we realize this and are too stubborn to even consider attitudinal adjustments that must be affective in order to become effective.

I must ask myself often, because I am often asked, how long women religious of solid character, deep spirituality, and gospel-oriented commitment will be made to feel like prodigals because they have chosen to symbolize their committed life by other than traditional or slightly modified traditional dress. How long shall we continue to emphasize the accidentals over substance and true integrity and commitment? As far-fetched as it may seem, Christ's most symbolic gesture was that he died without clothing and the clothing that he possessed was repossessed in a miniature gambling casino. How many schools have been left without women religious because bishops, priests, and laity considered them to be objects of obscenity when they gave up their religious garb? Have we swallowed the camel, been transfixed with the beam?

# RECRUITMENT AND FORMATION

All of what I have shared with you impacts tremendously on the present and future of religious life. The recruitment and formation of religious come into play here.

What kind of men and women are religious orders looking for today? What have we learned from our past, and what do we foresee for the future of religious life and for the Church as we search for these persons? Religious orders are looking for persons who are willing to take apostolic risks, persons who show creativity and are capable of learning from their experiences—successes as well as failures. They seek persons who are comfortable in working with the opposite sex and with lay persons, and who can live with a minimum of comfort. The Church needs and wants persons who see authority as a tremendous asset in mobilizing individual and corporate efforts for the building up of the kingdom, and not as a burden nor a security by which individuals and groups can abdicate their responsibilities. Persons are needed for whom vowed celibacy is an orientation to provide love that is trustworthy.

Religious communities cannot afford to attract nor accept safe, security-seeking, very conventional, or even reactionary types. The emphasis on recruitment is not merely to supply inexpensive laborers to staff our schools, hospitals, parishes, and retreat houses. Rather, it is to build the kingdom whose vision goes beyond our limited structures. Religious and those entering religious life need very much to be part of and contributing actors toward a vibrant, renewed, and renewing Church. Hence, they expect the hierarchy to welcome their collaboration; they expect the hierarchy to make itself aware of the purposes, ministries, and especially the talents that religious bring to the dioceses.

Practically speaking, religious desire very much to become privy to the research and planning of the dioceses in which they minister so that they may become partners in a shared vision in those matters that impact upon their own research and planning. Of course, the ideal would be joint planning by several religious communities with the dioceses and archdioceses. The reality, however, is that in all too many cases, religious communities are brought in after the fact. There is no question that religious communities often exacerbate the situation even further by planning for ministry in their own vacuum and often make diocesan planning inoperable. I suppose the bottom line here is that both bishops and religious should learn to recognize and build the kingdom with the full realization of their interdependence. Young men and women are attracted to religious life and give themselves to the building of the kingdom when they know they are joining a group that is a part of a vibrant, sharing, inclusive body. They will be willing to lower their nets after toiling all night. They will be happy to leave their boats at daybreak to follow a dream.

I want to close by quoting a portion of a letter written by a sister. She had just returned from an inter-American meeting of religious from Canada, the United States, and Latin America. Sr. Mary Jo says the following in speaking about vocations to the religious life.

> We are only beginning to realize the implications of choosing this prophetic way, a way that inevitably involves conflict and tension. My sense is that we are searching not so much for new theologies of religious life as for new ascetical practices that will make us fit for the long haul, that will sustain serenity in a swirl of accusations, that will shape us for the solitude and solidarity or struggle, that will constantly call us to celebrate in the midst of failure and fatigue. In short, we must discover practical patterns of countercultural living that go beyond the conservative nostalgia for the religious way of life that was a culture in itself and the liberal naiveté about the flaws of the sociocultural context in which we live.
>
> I have heard many of us at the meeting returning to our charisms, to the founding moments of our congregations, for inspiration in the prophetic way. We know that every founder and foundress who brought something new to the Church had moments of tension with the institutional Church. These times of tension were moments of birth and of hope. If history teaches us anything, it is that moments of conflict with the institutional Church were the best, not the worst, of times in religious congregations. Conflict is not merely something we cope with—it is part of our calling.

# VOCATIONS TO ORDAINED MINISTRY

## Daniel E. Pilarczyk
### Archbishop of Cincinnati

One way to deal with vocations to ordained ministry would be to put together one organic theological paper on orders in general and on the various manifestations of the theology of orders in three ranks. I have chosen, rather, to present three separable pieces which have some relationship to one another but are more like the distinct offerings on a standard symphony orchestra program. I offer a brief overture on episcopate, a concerto on diaconate, and a symphony on priesthood.

## EPISCOPATE

Catholic tradition has looked upon episcopate as the basic Holy Order. It contains and reflects the other two orders. The local bishop enjoys the fullness of the priesthood and is, at the same time, the head of the diaconate in his see. The old-time liturgists used to point to the various layers of vestments the bishop wore as a sign of this reality. In this brief overture, I wish to offer two themes on the vocation to episcopate that may in turn offer some insights into vocation to priesthood and diaconate.

*The call.* Like every ecclesiastical vocation, the vocation to episcopate is a call that is issued by the Church and ratified by the conferral of the sacrament of orders. The unique feature of the call to episcopate is its clarity. For many of us, it consisted in a *call* in the most literal sense. The telephone rings and a voice says, "The Nuncio wants to speak to you." But in every case, it is somehow clearly indicated that church authority wants *you* to be a bishop. You do not just sign up to become one. In fact, too much willingness to be a bishop is seen in most cases as an indication of unsuitability. In the other orders, the basic call of the Church is less obvious. It might be indicated by circumstances, or by personal abilities, or by the implicit word that local church authority is now taking applications. But in all cases, the call of the Church is presupposed for eligibility for the Sacrament of Holy Orders. A vocation is much more than a personal conviction that God wants you to do this. Without the intervention of church authority, there simply is no vocation.

*The need.* The number of bishops in the Church is limited by need, and that need must be demonstrated before church authority calls to episcopate. The vacancy of a canonically erected and viable see is one indication of need. In some cases, sees are suppressed or made titular when there is no longer a need for a residential bishop. In other cases (I understand this is happening in Italy), if sees are too small to need or support their own bishops, they are consolidated under one bishop. Most of us are also aware that the process of getting an auxiliary bishop appointed includes demonstrating the need for one. The supreme authorities in the Church are rightly concerned that there not be an excessive number of bishops. One is reminded of the song in the second act of Gilbert and Sullivan's *The Gondoliers*, which says,

> And bishops in their shovel hats
> Were plentiful as tabby cats—
> In point of fact, too many.

The lesson here is that it is not true that "more is better" when it comes to ordained ministers in the Church. Sometimes "more" is less good.

This concludes the overture on episcopate. Its themes may be helpful later in our discussions.

# DIACONATE

My concerto on diaconate has three brief movements. The brevity should not be construed as a sign of the subject's unimportance, but as a reflection of the demands of the principal subject of my presentation which is yet to come. I present here some history of the diaconate, an overview of authoritative sources about diaconate, and a list of questions that contemporary reality suggests on the matter.

*Some history.* The sixth chapter of Acts recounts the apostles' call of seven men of good reputation to deal with the distribution of food to the Hellenistic widows so that the apostles could continue to devote themselves to prayer and the service of the Word. Even if this was actually an ordination to what became presbyterate, as some theologians think,[1] deacons appear in the New Testament by the time of the letter to the Philippians 1:1 and the first letter to Timothy (ch. 3).

In the postapostolic writings, we read of deacons in the traditional ministries of word, sacrament, and charity. They also seem to have been leaders in some rural communities, temporal administrators, and personal envoys of bishops. By the fourth century, however, the diaconate began to go into decline, apparently due to tensions between deacons and presbyters and bishops. Gradually the diaconate was limited to liturgical functions and eventually became merely a step to the priesthood.

Vatican II, in *Lumen Gentium*, 29, called for the restoration of the permanent diaconate and gave a special emphasis to their fittingness in mission lands.[2] Pope Paul VI restored the permanent diaconate in 1967,[3] and in 1968, the American hierarchy requested and was granted permission to begin ordaining men to this order in the United States. We now have some 7,500 permanent deacons in our country, roughly as many as the number of religious brothers and, I believe, more than the rest of the world combined. It is worth mentioning that missionary bishops generally did not implement the restoration of the diaconate, apparently because they feared the submergence of the ministry of catechist in their jurisdictions.

*What we know about diaconate.* Official church teaching on the diaconate is quite limited. This is due in part, I believe, to its brief history, both ancient and modern. Such a situation provides an interesting example of the influence of experience on theology. Brief experience makes for little theology. The *locus classicus* is *Lumen Gentium*, 29. Here the Council

---

1. See Jean Galot, SJ, *Theology of the Priesthood* (San Francisco: 1984), 160ff.

2. *Ad Gentes*, 16.

3. See Motu Proprio *Sacrum Diaconatus Ordinem*.

speaks of "a lower level of the hierarchy" than priests, "upon whom hands are imposed 'not unto priesthood but unto a ministry of service.'" "They serve the people of God in the ministry of the liturgy, of the word, and of charity. It is the duty of the deacon . . . to administer baptism solemnly, to be custodian and dispenser of the Eucharist, to assist at and bless marriages in the name of the Church, to bring Viaticum to the dying, to read the sacred Scripture to the faithful, to instruct and exhort the people, to preside at the worship and prayer of the faithful, to administer sacramentals, and to officiate at funeral and burial services." At the end of this long list of duties comes mention of deacons as dedicated to duties of charity and administration.

In the next paragraph, the Council calls for the restoration of the diaconate and its availability to married men, principally because the duties outlined earlier "can in many areas be fulfilled only with difficulty according to the prevailing discipline of the Latin Church." The Council in this section quotes Hippolytus, *Apostolic Tradition* 1,9: "not unto priesthood but unto a ministry of service." This quote has become a kind of thumbnail description of diaconate in our times. I think it is worth pointing out that the full quotation reads, ". . . only the bishop lays hands on the deacon. He is ordained not for the priesthood but for the service of the bishop, to carry out his orders." If this reflects authentic tradition, then the deacon is not the subordinate of the priest in his ministry but of the bishop, even if his diaconal ministry consists in collaboration with priests on the bishop's orders.

I find that much of the other authoritative material on the nature of diaconate is a repetition of *Lumen Gentium*. Pope Paul VI in *Sacrum Diaconatus Ordinem* provides an additional insight, though, when he says that the sign value of *ordained* diaconate as a ministry of service is "so that those who are called to it can *permanently* [*stabiliter*] serve the mysteries of Christ and the Church."[4]

As presented to us by the Council, therefore, the deacon is distinguished not so much by special functions as by a permanent commitment to service or assistance to the bishop and, at the behest of the bishop, to the presbyterate and the Church at large.

*What we do not know about diaconate.* As is the case with anything new, even if the newness is only *quoad nos*, there

---

4. SDO, Introduction (emphasis added).

are lots of unanswered questions about the restored diaconate. Some are questions of theory, some are questions of practice:

- If the diaconate is fundamentally a function of service, what does that say about the role of priest? Of bishop? Whom is the deacon supposed to serve?
- What does it mean for deacons to be clerics?
- What is the significance of the fact that those who are promoting the ordination of women generally seem to focus on priesthood rather than on diaconate?
- What is the significance of the large number of men who have presented themselves for training for the diaconate and the large number of ordained permanent deacons in our country?
- What is the relationship between permanent deacons and full-time lay pastoral ministers?
- What does the fact that most permanent deacons in our country serve the Church in part-time, unpaid positions signify?

As we deal with the question of vocations, it is clear that we are not dealing with dearth in the permanent diaconate but with abundance. I believe we do not yet know what such abundance means. Perhaps one way to come to grips with this question is to keep ourselves attentive as time goes by to the gifts which the permanent diaconate brings to our country, and to ask ourselves what the Church in the United States would be like if we were to learn that the permanent diaconate would be suppressed tomorrow.

## PRIESTHOOD

I have called this section of my presentation a symphony not only because it is the major item on the program, but also because it is divided into four movements or sections. First, I wish to offer a contemporary (though admittedly incomplete and personal) phenomenology of ordained priesthood. Next, I will present the theology of priesthood which I perceive to be inherent in the teachings of the Second Vatican Council. The third section will be a consideration of celibacy and priesthood. The finale will be a series of thoughts about where we might go from here in our concern for priestly vocations. I am presuming in this presentation that the basic priestly function is that of parish priest, and that other priestly works are validated by analogy with parish ministry. I acknowledge throughout that there are other ways in which to treat these matters.

Moreover, I cannot say everything. There are two reasons for this. One is that we do not have time. The other is that I do not know everything about priesthood. Probably nobody does short of the Lord himself. Even having said that, I find myself as I begin this presentation remembering a remark of Virgil. Augustus wrote to Virgil while he was working on the *Aeneid* asking for news of the epic. How was it going? The poet responded that the task was so great, he must have agreed to take it on in a fit of mental aberration.[5] I share those sentiments as I begin.

## A Phenomenology

I entered the seminary on September 2, 1948. I was fourteen years old and in my second year of high school. At that point in the Church's history in our country, the image of the priest was clear and bright. He was *the* minister in the Church, *the* church person. There was no other, except perhaps for religious sisters, who were taken mostly for granted by fourteen-year-old boys. The priest dealt with sacred matters in a sacred language. He was versed in the mysteries of the faith. He was holy by the mere fact of being priest. He was highly educated and wise and had unquestioned authority in every facet of the parish. It did not matter much if he could not preach very well. The really important thing was that he could celebrate Mass.

The specifics of his personal life were shrouded in mystery. He seemed happy, and he seemed to live better that most of the parishioners. That was no problem because, after all, he was the priest.

To be a priest was the highest life a boy could aspire to. It meant being a *real* Christian; it meant being called to serve Christ and his Church; it meant being respected and revered almost as Christ himself. The possibility of having a vocation was a shining opportunity for a young boy at a time when opportunities were few.

Some sacrifices were required, but in 1948 sacrifices were part of life. We were old enough to remember the end of the Depression and all of World War II. From some points of view,

5. "*Tanta incohata res est ut paene vitio mentis tantum opus ingressus mihi videar.*" Recorded in Macrobius, *Saturnalia,* 1, 24.

the priesthood was a hard life, but all of life was or had been hard for virtually everybody in those days. Celibacy was not much of a question for candidates to the priesthood then, because we all had at least one unmarried aunt or uncle; and besides, we knew it was God's will for priests to remain without wife and family.

In the process of seminary education, our image of the priest underwent some modifications. It was deepened and refined, but essentially it remained the image of the sacred leader, the man set apart.

Since the Second Vatican Council, this image has changed. Today, the priesthood is perceived as one ministry among many. Its nature is questioned. The traditional requirement of celibacy is under attack. Priests find themselves asking, "Why does the Church need me? What do I do that someone else could not?" Since the Council, thousands of priests have abandoned their commitment to priestly ministry, and some of those who have remained are overworked, unhappy, and embittered.

In the past, bishops and priests *were* the Church; and its word—their word—was law. Lay people now perceive that they, too, are the Church. Almost everybody has something to be angry about in today's Church, or at least something to say about it. The pastor, formerly solitary and supreme, now deals with a pastoral staff, with lay teachers in the school, a parish council, a finance committee, an education commission, and a liturgy commission. In addition, he reads that people are leaving his church by the hundreds because his sermons are so unappealing, and that he has been grossly derelict in his duty to reach out to the increasing numbers of the unchurched.

The image of the priest has changed in the Church. It is almost as if priesthood is a different office now, except that nobody is too sure where the difference really lies.

But the Church has not changed in a vacuum. The world has changed, too. It seems to have become increasingly unfriendly to organized religion, far less tolerant of cultic figures. Formal religious practice is on the decline. Church attendance, even for many who claim to be church members, has become a matter of occasional personal choice.

Life expectations have changed, as well. People now claim the right to success and comfort. They look for more from society, from government, from their jobs, from their personal relationships, from education. A life of self-sacrifice was once looked upon as an inspiring human achievement; it now has about it the aura of personal failure.

Sexual attitudes have also changed. A basic unspoken presumption of our society is that everyone has the right to as much sexual activity as he or she can get and of whatever kind he or she prefers. (If you do not believe this, watch prime time TV for a week, or study the letters to the editor during the next pornography case that comes up in your town.) The celibate life, far from being a value, is seen as outmoded, unjustly imposed on priestly ministers by an obscurantist Church. Or, it is seen as a screen to hide behind for those with atypical sexual inclinations.

These last years have been a time of unprecedented upheaval in both the Church and the world. In view of this, it is no wonder that *fewer* young men are presenting themselves to serve the Church in the self-sacrificing celibate life of the priest. The wonder may be that there are any at all.

It is my perception that there are two main issues about priesthood that have arisen from this turbulence. One is the nature and purpose of ordained priestly ministry in a renewing Church. The other is the meaning of priestly celibacy in today's world. I would like to consider each of these.

## The Theology of Priesthood of Vatican II

Vatican II offers the most recent and most authoritative teaching about the nature of the Church and the roles of its ministers. For that reason, I have chosen to base my treatment of the theology of priesthood on the documents of the Council.

I begin with the Council's teaching about bishops. It is a clear and straightforward teaching. The bishop is the head, the leader, of the local Church. As *Lumen Gentium* states: "Bishops have taken up the service of the community, presiding in place of God over the flock whose shepherds they are, as teachers of doctrine, priests of sacred worship, and officers of good order" (20). "The individual bishop . . . is the visible principle and foundation of unity in his particular church, fashioned after the model of the universal Church. . . . The individual bishops . . . exercise pastoral government over the portion of the People of God committed to their care" (23). There is no question about the role of bishop in the Church.

The basic role of the priest, according to the Council, is to extend the work of the bishop to a portion of the diocese. He is to be the *alter ego* of the bishop. Over and over again the Council speaks of priests, including religious priests, as helpers of or collaborators with the bishop in his pastoral office. I have counted at least ten such *loci*.[6] Priests participate in the ministry of the bishop.[7] They make the bishop present in the local congregation.[8] They depend on the bishop in the exercise of their authority.[9] Pastors take the place of the bishop.[10]

And just as the ministry of the bishop is the service of leadership, so also is the ministry of the priest. Priests exercise the function of Christ as shepherd and head within the limits of their authority.[11] By ordination priests "are so configured to Christ the Priest that they can act in the person of Christ the Head."[12] Spiritual power is conferred on the priest for the upbuilding of the Church.[13] Priests are "rulers of the community"[14] and the faithful should follow them as their shepherds and fathers.[15]

Priests exercise this participation in the bishop's role, this mission of leadership, the Council says, in the same triple ministry which is the bishop's: that of preaching the Gospel, shepherding the faithful, and celebrating divine worship.[16] Moreover, the office of pastors is not confined to the care of the faithful as individuals, but is also properly extended to the formation of a genuine Christian community.[17] The center of priestly ministry is the celebration of the Eucharist, because the Eucharist is "the source and apex of the whole work of preaching the Gospel,"[18] is the "basis and center" of Christian community,[19] and "contains the Church's entire spiritual wealth."[20]

Thus spoke Vatican II on ministerial priesthood. Its prime

---

6. *Lumen Gentium*, 20, 21, 28; *Christus Dominus*, 11, 15, 30, 34 (religious); *Presbyterorum Ordinis*, 2, 7, 12.

7. LG, 28, 41.

8. LG, 28.

9. CD, 15; PO, 6.

10. *Sacrosanctum Concilium*, 42.

11. LG, 28; PO, 5.

12. PO, 2, 12.

13. PO, 6.

14. PO, 13.

15. PO, 9.

16. LG, 28.

17. PO, 6.

18. PO, 5.

19. PO, 6.

20. PO, 5.

analog is episcopate, and it can only be properly understood as a participation in the pastoral leadership of the bishop. This is not to say that priests are mere stand-ins for bishops. Priests have their own proper role, but it is a role of pastoral leadership as is the role of the bishop.

I would now like to clarify this teaching by three further considerations that bear on areas of confusion about the nature of priesthood. I will have to be briefer than the subject matter would demand—suggestive (in the Italian sense!) rather than exhaustive.

The first consideration is that of the relationship between ordained priesthood and the common priesthood of all the faithful. The two are different in essence and not only in degree.[21] It is not that the ordained priest has *more* of the priesthood of the faithful. He has a different kind of priesthood. The difference lies in both the source and the purpose of each. The source of the common priesthood of all the faithful is ultimately the action of Christ, the model of sanctity for every human being, in the sacrament of baptism. The source of the ordained priesthood is the action of Christ, the head of the Church, in the sacrament of orders. These are two distinct actions of Christ exercised for two different purposes. The purpose of the common priesthood is to offer spiritual sacrifices and proclaim the power of Christ, to participate in the sacraments, to offer prayer and thanksgiving, to give witness to the world by a holy life, and to engage in self-denial and active charity.[22] The ordained priest, on the other hand, "molds and rules the priestly people."[23]

The universal priesthood of Christians is called upon primarily to contribute to the sanctification of the world. The offering of spiritual sacrifices is not aimed only at promoting individual perfection, but is an intercession and a witness on behalf of all human beings. The universal priesthood seeks primarily to enhance the holiness of the universe.

The ordained priesthood, on the other hand, exists primarily for service within the Church. It has for its purpose to minister to the universal priesthood, to promote its exercise. The ministerial priesthood is never an end in itself, nor does the universal priesthood exist to sustain the ordained priesthood. "Those ministers who are endowed with sacred powers

---

21. LG, 10.
22. LG, 10.
23. LG, 10.

are servants of their brethren, so that all who are of the People of God, and therefore enjoy a true Christian dignity, can work toward a common goal freely and in an orderly way, and arrive at salvation."[24] That common goal is the sanctification of the world. If we cannot understand priesthood without understanding episcopate, we can understand neither episcopate nor priesthood unless we also understand laity.

The second clarifying consideration has to do with the idea of leadership. We have seen that Vatican II speaks of priests in terms of presiding, of headship, of spiritual power, of ruler, of shepherd, of father. Vatican II does not speak of the priest in terms of boss, of master, or of monarch. The kind of leadership that is involved with priesthood, and which the various terms used by Vatican II try to describe, is a very special one. It involves authority from Christ and the Church, to be sure, but also a respect for the lay calling of those it serves and a willingness to take advantage for the community of the gifts and talents of all its members. It involves an awareness that the priest exists for his people and not vice versa. It involves a conviction that the parish exists in order to enable lay people to be lay people in the world, not to take them out of the world for exclusive service to the parish. It involves real, affective love and concern for parishioners.

The leadership of the priest does not mean exclusivity of ministry, either. Others can be called to direct service in the local Christian community, and the priest needs to see them not as rivals or surrogates, but as authentic collaborators in the Lord's work for his people.

It may well be that one of the most difficult problems of today's Church lies in finding a way to affirm and maintain the real, authentic leadership role of the ordained priest without downplaying the true gifts and responsibilities of lay persons, who have now for twenty years been taught that they have a rightful role to play in the life of the Church. The problem lies in being a good shepherd without treating people like sheep, in being a loving father without treating people like children. It may be a crisis of metaphors, but the tension is real.

The third clarifying consideration has to do with sacramental character. We do not hear much about the three sacramental characters any more. Perhaps the idea of a permanent imprint on the soul is too material for people today. Perhaps

---

24. LG, 19.

there are other theological currents at work. But I think the truth expressed by the teaching is an important one, and one that needs to be reaffirmed in our time.

When the Council of Trent taught authoritatively that orders imprint a character,[25] I believe it wanted to ensure that the Church would teach that the priesthood is not just a specialized function in the Church, a job that could be filled as needed and then abandoned. Rather than being a job exercised by selected laymen, the priesthood is a specialized, permanent participation in the life of Christ. Whatever the sociological realities may be these days, the priest is simply not "just like everybody else." In fact, it is a matter of faith that he is different from everybody else. He is an unchangeable sign or sacrament of the love of Christ the Head for his Church.

Is the priest for that reason somehow better than everyone else? I do not think so. In fact, ordained priesthood makes no sense except in the context of the Church entire and in the context of service to lay persons for whose benefit the Church primarily exists. We need to continue to analyze what we are saying if we choose to speak of higher or more perfect vocations in the Church. But the fact remains that ordained priesthood is a different way of being in the Church, so different that it definitively changes the one on whom it is conferred. We neglect that truth at our peril.

To sum, the ordained priest shares the function of the bishop and is therefore pastor, father, and leader to the portion of the diocese entrusted to him. He is there to teach, to sanctify, to unify the people and so enable them to carry out the implications of their common priesthood in the world. He is charged with this pastoral responsibility through a special conformation to Christ in sacred orders. This change is permanent and is directed totally to the strengthening of the community and the building up of the Church.

And that brings us to celibacy.

## Priestly Celibacy

Let me begin by observing that I am addressing here only the discipline of celibacy for diocesan priests in the Western Church. The scriptural *locus classicus* on celibacy is Matthew 19:10ff. Jesus has been talking about the indissolubility of marriage, and the apostles say, "If that's the way things are, it is better not to marry." Jesus says, "Well, that is not for every-

---

25. Cf. Denzinger-Schöenmetzer 1767, 1774.

body either. Remaining unmarried may be better, but only for those who have received a special gift from God. These are the ones who are eunuchs for the sake of the kingdom of heaven. If someone is able to embrace this gift, he should do so by all means."[26]

Historically, celibacy for the kingdom has always been highly regarded in the Church. Over the centuries, the Church of the West has made dedication to celibacy a defining precondition for ordination to priesthood.

Vatican II dealt with celibacy in *Presbyterorum Ordinis*, 16, and *Lumen Gentium*, 42. Both these sections speak of celibacy principally in terms of pastoral availability. Celibacy "signifies and stimulates pastoral charity. . . . [Through celibacy priests] more easily hold fast to [Christ] with undivided heart. They more freely devote themselves to him and through him to the service of God and men. They more readily minister to his kingdom and to the work of heavenly regeneration, and thus become more apt to exercise paternity in Christ, and do so to a greater extent."[27]

In 1967, Pope Paul VI issued his encyclical *Sacerdotalis Coelibatus*. There he offered three reasons for the celibacy of priests. The first is Christological.[28] Celibates image Christ in a special way in that they reflect Christ's own exclusive dedication to the kingdom by sharing his very condition of living. The second reason is ecclesiological.[29] The celibate loves and dedicates himself to all the children of God. He is best disposed for a continuous exercise of a perfect charity. The third reason lies in the eschatological significance of celibacy.[30] It proclaims the presence on earth of the final stage of salvation where our life is hidden with Christ in God.

I would like to try to say in my own words what I think the commitment to celibacy is all about in the Church, but first a reminder. The controversy about priestly celibacy is not new in the Church. It has been around at least since the Spanish Council of Elvira in 306. It took centuries to achieve universal application of the discipline in the Western Church. It was discussed again and again at general councils: Lateran II (1139), Lateran IV (1215), Vienne (1311–12), Constance (1414–

---

26. Cf. J. P. Meier, *Matthew* (Wilmington, Del.: Michael Glazier, 1980), 216ff.

27. PO, 16.

28. *Sacerdotalis Coelibatus*, 19–25.

29. SC, 26–32.

30. SC, 33–34.

18), Florence (1431–45), Lateran V (1512–17), and Trent (1545–63). The discipline was reaffirmed by Vatican II.

The question of celibacy is one that will not die, perhaps because there is no apodictic, rational proof that things have to be that way, or even that they should be that way. There is no essential, inherent connection between priesthood and celibacy that would make their separation absurd. And yet, at the most solemn moments of the Church's teaching and legislating activity (i.e., at general councils), the Church's leadership consistently has come down in favor of celibacy as a condition for priesthood. A cynic might say that it is merely a case of the bishops trying to maintain control over their priests. Someone else might say, though, that it is the Spirit guiding Christ's Church in its own often incomprehensible ways. It may also be that the charismatic kernel of priestly celibacy manifests itself differently at different times and so requires a constant effort of identification and explanation. In any case, we are not the first bishops in the history of the Church to face the question of the connection between celibacy and priesthood.

What is the Church trying to say, then, when it determines that priests must be celibate? I would like to start from secular human experience. It is not unreasonable, though it is not common, for people to be so taken up with certain values as to want nothing else for their lives. They do not say that other values are bad, but only that they themselves wish to give all *their* energies to a specific human good—politics, science, the arts, sports. In the lives of people like this, there is room for only one major commitment, not because of the smallness of their lives but because of the size of that one commitment.

It was not too long ago that most large families had at least one child who chose not to marry so that he or she could take care of the parents as they grew older. I suspect you have had people ask you, as they have asked me, why they never hear any preaching in church on the value of the single life in the world. Remaining unmarried for a specific purpose is not monstrous or unreasonable.

The New Testament (Mt 19ff.) speaks of those who remain unmarried for the sake of Christ and his kingdom. This is not for everyone. It is a special gift given to some for the good of the Church at large. Such people are so enchanted, so fascinated by Christ and his kingdom, so caught up in their spell that they do not want to do anything else but work directly for Christ and the kingdom. They want their lives to be completely available for apostolic service. In the process of living out this dedication to Christ and the Church, they image him in a unique way. They offer special energies to the life of the Church. They teach with their lives that there is a future way of living in which everyone will be fully and definitively taken up in Christ.

Here we are in the realm of charismatic enthusiasm. It is not so much a matter of giving up marriage for the sake of giving up something as it is a matter of extraordinary joy at finding a different treasure. The Western Church has decided over the centuries that men of this type, and they only, would be ordained priests. Few in numbers? Perhaps. A fitting decision? I believe so.

Having said this, though, we have not yet said everything. I would now like to offer five caveats about celibacy and the way it is understood.

First, it is not the case that people have a vocation to the priesthood and then the Church forces them to be celibate. Vocations come from a certain combination of human and divine gifts *and* from the discernment and call of the Church through the bishop. The Church's leadership over the centuries has discerned that only those with the gift of celibacy should be called to priesthood. Logically, celibacy comes first, then priesthood. The two are separable things. We do not force priests to be celibate. We only invite those who are committed to celibacy to be priests. Psychologically, it may happen the other way around. Men first become attracted to the priesthood and then consent to a life of celibacy because of the Church's law. But even in these instances, the commitment to celibacy comes before priesthood is conferred.

In this context, I would observe that when we speak of "the gift of celibacy" we can do so in two senses. From one point of view, it is a charismatic gift from God to certain individuals. From another, it is a gift from the candidate to the Church, viz., a pledge of a lifetime of full and individual ministerial witness and service to God's people. The Church has discerned that only those who are willing and able to offer this gift to the Church should be ordained to priesthood.

I would also observe that the very real pain, burdens, and frustration that sometimes come with celibacy are not necessarily a sign that it is a man-made burden, unjustly imposed. All God's gifts, beginning with life itself, are heavy.

Second caveat: Celibacy does not downplay matrimony. Such would be the case if being a priest were in and of itself and always better than being a lay person. If being a priest is "better" than being a lay person, and if you cannot be married and be a priest, then something is wrong with marriage. In fact, as I have said earlier, ordained priesthood exists for the sake of the Church at large and cannot be properly envisaged except as a service to the People of God. (Note that Vatican II and other recent church teaching about celibacy do not speak of cultic purity—a purity arising from sexual abstinence—on the part of the priest.)

Third, celibacy is not so much a giving up, a discipline, but a style of life, indeed a style of loving. It is primarily positive. It implies an intensity in the focus of the celibate's psychic energies. The portion of the church community entrusted to the priest is to play something of the same role in his life that family plays in the lives of married persons. Celibacy needs affective expression. It is not true that the celibate gives up human affection. On the contrary, the celibate priest should be able to say, "I love my people, and I do not love anybody else as much," and he should be able to say this as sincerely and straightforwardly as a married man would say it about his wife and children. In fact, *Presbyterorum Ordinis*, 14, tells us that the bond of priestly perfection which unifies the life and activity of the priest is nothing other than pastoral love.[31] (This is not to deny, of course, that the priest requires the support of intimate friends beyond the limits of his ministry.)

Fourth, celibacy is not a gift that comes all packaged and wrapped, requiring only to be used. Rather, celibacy is a willingness to risk, to risk everything on the direct service of Christ and the Church. It is a wager that the celibate makes on the validity of his work for the kingdom. It is not a guarantee, but a call, a challenge, an opportunity. It requires constant attention and constant nourishment and development through contact with the Lord in prayer and through deliberate and explicit personal dedication to priestly ministry. Consequently, it is possible to cheat on celibacy, not just by sexual activity, but by self-indulgence, by selfishly limiting one's availability, by making the priesthood a job instead of a love affair.

Fifth caveat: Changing the Church's policy of ordaining only celibates to priesthood could bring with it as many problems as it proposes to solve. These problems include those of financial support, of mobility, of numbers, of marriage strain

---

31. Cf. PO, 15ff.

and divorce, of tension between married and celibate priests. What effects would come from the necessary sense of loss which parishioners would feel as they learn that the priest is no longer *theirs* in the same way he was before? What implications about the Church's teaching on human sexuality, matrimony, and, indeed, on the nature of priesthood itself lie hidden in such a change?

In sum, a case can be made for priestly celibacy. It is not the case that can be made for a geometry theorem, but rather the case that can be made for falling in love, for falling so in love with Christ and the service of his Church that one is willing to take the position that nothing else in life really matters.

## Where Do We Go from Here?

A lot has happened since I entered the seminary on that September afternoon in 1948. The Church has changed. The world has changed. The image of priest is different. The number of seminary candidates has declined. Our local churches continue to need priestly ministers. What are we to think? What are we to do? I would like to offer a list of seven considerations, with the hope that our discussion will surface many more.

1. Can we arrive at a clear and widely accepted theology of lay ministry in the Church? If everything the lay person does in virtue of his or her baptism is ministry, how is the priest's ministry different? Is he merely the cultic figure, the sacramental circuit rider? Or is it rather the case that lay ministry, in the strict sense, is a participation in the work of the Church's shepherds and requires some kind of specific authorization from them? Is it enough merely to say that we are dealing with different ecclesiologies in the one Church?

2. How can we get abroad stories of happy and successful priests? I am convinced that the best recruiters for our seminaries are productive and happy priests who know what they are all about. Enthusiasm is caught, not taught.

3. How can we bishops offer more affective and effective support and respect to our priests? It is a tough life out there. We know that, but do they know we know that? How do you tell a thirty-five-year veteran that you love him and you need him, or a fifteen-month rookie who is beginning to wonder what he has gotten himself into?

4. Is there any comfort to be derived for anybody from the

possibility that we are in the midst of a historical transition from a time when priests did everything to a new situation when others are involved in ministry? If we had the same number of priests per capita today that we used to have, would we now have permanent deacons and full-time lay ministers? Is it possible that we might have had too many priests in the past?

5. What would happen to the Church if every priest nourished his celibate ministry with thirty or forty minutes of contemplative prayer each day? What would happen if every priest nourished his celibate ministry with healthy, mature relationships with ordained, vowed, married, single friends? What would happen if every priest knew how to let himself be loved by those he serves?

6. What, for that matter, would happen to the Church if prayer for priestly vocations became a regular part of the prayer life of each parishioner? Jesus gives us a very clear directive about recruiting vocations: "Pray the Lord of the harvest to send out laborers into his harvest" (Mt 9:38). Could such prayer result in more frequent explicit encouragement toward priesthood on the part of parents and teachers? Might it at least help them to ask themselves if they are actually discouraging vocations?

7. How can we say in some convincing fashion that the abolition of the condition of celibacy and the ordination of women are not, practically speaking, open questions, and that what is really needed is attention to the problems at hand through means—such as prayer, penance, and personal encouragement—we already have at our disposal?

It is clear that we are in some kind of a crisis of priestly ministry. The nature of the crisis is not all that clear. Is it a crisis of image? A crisis of numbers? A crisis of celibacy? A crisis of change? A crisis of lay ministries? A crisis of prayer? A crisis of secularism? A crisis of confidence? It is probably all of these, and perhaps other things as well. And, we have to respond to the crisis.

But, is it not also possible, given the strange and sneaky way in which God loves us, that somehow at the bottom there may also lurk a blessing?

# AND NOW, WHAT NEXT?

## Joseph Cardinal Bernardin
## Archbishop of Chicago

I would like to begin on a personal note. In April of this year I celebrated the twentieth anniversary of my episcopal ordination. During that time, I have served as auxiliary bishop of a small archdiocese, Ordinary of a medium-sized archdiocese, and, more recently, Ordinary of a huge archdiocese. In between, or concurrently, I have served as general secretary and president of the National Conference of Catholic Bishops. Because of my responsibilities and experience, I attach importance to a number of issues. But none is of greater concern to me than the topic we have been discussing—namely, vocations, and, in particular, ecclesial vocations. I spend a considerable amount of time working with men and women who promote and nourish church vocations, both during the recruitment and formation phases and later when they are actually in ministry. I speak about this topic, therefore, with great conviction—as I know you do.

## THEOLOGY OF VOCATION

It was important, I believe, that we began with Cardinal Law's paper. From remarks I heard throughout the week, I think many of us were eager to begin discussing how we

85

might turn around the declining number of candidates for the priesthood and religious life. This touches us directly and immediately. But our approach would be superficial unless we first situate the immediate crisis within the broader context of the vocation of all Christians. Without a sound theology of vocation, we will think more in terms of specific programs and strategies than in terms of the deeper mystery that is at work in all Christians. Unless the functional dimension of our efforts is rooted in the deeper relational realities, we may never get to the heart of the problem.

Cardinal Law defined vocation as "the call to experience and live life as pure gift" and, in turn, "as a gift of self, as sacrificial love." The crisis, he said, stems from the fact that many are refusing this call. He identified the vocation crisis as a crisis of faith. In response to some comments, he indicated that the refusal was not necessarily due to an outright denial but to a weakening of faith in Christ and his paschal mystery that causes people to hold back or to choose other values. Many cultural factors contribute to this hesitancy or refusal: consumerism, materialism, narcissism, a practical if not a conceptual atheism, a general unwillingness to make permanent commitments.

The discussion of Cardinal Law's talk, as I understood it, highlighted the fact that the causes of the vocation crisis are complex, and so our analyses must be nuanced. For example, there is evidence of generosity and sacrificial love on the part of many faith-filled young people who would be good candidates for priesthood and religious life, but they seem less interested in making this kind of commitment than was the case in the recent past. Then, there is the developmental aspect of vocations: Even though one makes a permanent commitment at the time of ordination, religious profession, or marriage, it takes time to *grow* into the vocation, time to understand, and to realize its full meaning and potential. This has many implications for the way we minister to our priests, religious, and laity.

We agreed that, in light of this situation, there is a great need for *evangelization* aimed at conversion, a dynamic conversion of mind and heart. Such evangelization and conversion—such renewal of personal and ecclesial life—must be the basis for specific programs and strategies aimed at increasing church vocations. Otherwise, the programs will have minimal effect.

I hope we will leave Collegeville determined to pursue the development of a sound theology of vocation, with all its theoretical and practical implications, as the basis for our vocational work in the future. Such a theology must explore Christian vocation in its many dimensions, drawing from anthropology, Christology, ecclesiology, and sacramental theology.

This theology of vocation, of course, must be applied. To put it another way, *vocation* does not exist in a vacuum. It is *people* who have vocations; it is people who are called. And as pastors, we must help identify, support, and nourish vocations to lay leadership, priesthood, and religious life. At any given moment, one particular group may need more attention than another but, overall, our approach must be comprehensive and holistic.

## LAY LEADERSHIP AND MINISTRY

I wish to commend Archbishop Pilarczyk for one of the most lucid explanations I have ever heard of the difference between the universal priesthood of the faithful, in which we all participate in virtue of baptism, and the ministerial priesthood, to which one is called by the Church and in which one participates through ordination. Without this understanding, there will be only confusion when we speak about the mission of the laity to the world, lay ministry, the unique ministry of the ordained, and the relationship that exists among these three. It is essential that we understand the difference ourselves, that we use precise language when we talk about these realities, and that we do all we can to make sure that others understand.

Bishop Lucker's paper on lay leadership elicited a strong positive response. Almost all the comments affirmed the importance of distinguishing between the vocation (or responsibility) of the laity to transform and renew the world and their call to participate in ecclesial ministries. The word *ministry* seems more appropriate for the latter; the former is more properly called *discipleship, witness*, etc.

There seems to be widespread agreement that, while Vatican II made the distinctions and emphasized the importance of both, more attention has been given during the past twenty years to the formation of people for *ecclesial* ministries. While we must continue to develop lay ecclesial ministries, more attention must be given to providing the formation, support, and encouragement needed by the laity to fulfill their responsibility to the world. It was noted that as Catholics become more affluent, they sometimes become less disposed to challenge the societal structures that undermine gospel values. By *world* or *society*, we mean the various spheres in which lay people live and work: the family, the professions, the workplace, civic society, and so forth. We must assist and support them in their task of bringing the gospel message to the world, but we should not try to *control* them. We must trust them to use their talents in creative and effective ways, even though this may involve some risk.

In the final analysis, the laity must experience conversion before they can succeed in fulfilling their vocation to transform the world. As pastors, we can facilitate the discharge of their responsibility in many ways:

- by our willingness to truly *listen* to them (there is, of course, the correlative obligation on our part to teach, and sometimes there exists a gap between their "lived experience" and our magisterial teaching);
- by providing theological and spiritual formation by becoming, through our ministry of word and sacrament and through our example, the instruments through which they experience conversion;
- by a willingness to "let go" and not try to control or direct their initiatives or to "clericalize" them;
- by supporting family life, which is so essential to nurturing vocations;
- by developing parishes as welcoming communities that witness and nourish faith;
- by developing a more positive, richer theology of sexuality, one that will elicit more assent and less dissent (such a theology of sexuality has important implications for the lived experience of both the sacrament of marriage and the commitment of celibacy).

What about those who are called to ecclesial ministry, those who are called to be authentic collaborators with us in the ministry of the Church? There has been an explosion of lay ministry in recent years. This has been a great asset, but it has also caused *tensions*. One cause of tension has been a lack of clarity regarding the difference between ordained and lay ministry. Only when there is greater clarity will priests feel less threatened and be better disposed and able to affirm the laity in their gifts and leadership. The role of women in the Church and society, in general, and in the ministry, in particular, has been another source of tension. Both issues constitute a challenge we must address positively and creatively. We need to develop more effective criteria for identifying, forming, certifying, and designating lay ministers. We must also seriously consider providing adequate compensation for lay ministers and establish a constructive, positive balance or relationship between paid ministers and volunteers.

## RELIGIOUS LIFE

I am sure that if our discussion about religious life had taken place two or three years ago, it would have been quite different. The reason is the study of religious life in which the Holy Father asked us to participate. Several years ago, while giving religious full credit for all they have done for the Church, our discussion would have taken on more of a "we–they" character. Now I perceive a greater sense of solidarity with our religious brothers and sisters. I detect a shift from preoccupation with defining religious life to a concern about how we might integrate religious more fully into the life and ministry of the churches over which we preside. My dialogue with religious prompts me to think that there has also been a significant shift among religious—a shift in consciousness regarding their identity and their mission to the world. These shifts, I believe, have created a critical moment for religious, and the well-being of religious and the Church at large depends in great measure on how we respond.

An essential need, as almost everyone agrees, is to continue the dialogue. It must be broadened, however, so as to include our priests and laity—especially priests. One of the tensions for women religious is their relationship with priests. There are several reasons for this. Because of existing structures, many women must depend on priests in terms of their ministry, vocations, etc. In many instances, too, women religious have engaged more intensely in personal and ecclesial renewal than priests. This has caused differences in outlook and attitude, giving rise to misunderstandings and conflict. The overall decrease in the number of religious, the emergence of new ministries, and the resulting decrease in the number of religious engaged in traditional ministries (such as teaching) have only exacerbated the situation. We must attend quickly to this alienation.

We also must intensify our efforts to collaborate with religious within our dioceses. We must continue to give them a greater voice in diocesan planning and priorities. The trend to invite them to assume significant leadership positions is important and welcome. We must also discuss the financial difficulty some communities experience because of their aging members and, together, search for solutions.

I have just completed the dialogue sessions requested by the Pontifical Commission. I'd like to share with you the questions I have already put on our agenda in Chicago for future sessions: "How can we establish collaboration among religious, laity, and diocesan clergy as a normal mode of contemporary apostolic action? How can we develop a vision for the future that will include creative options and apostolic risk when vocations are growing fewer? How can we encourage a community to develop in such a way as to be securely identifiable and attractive to young candidates? How can we support you in maintaining high standards for admission to your communities when decreasing numbers tempt us to take more chances with personal needs of applicants?"

One final point: I agree completely with those who say that the way the Holy See responds to our reports on the study of religious life is crucial. It is important, I believe, that through the Conference we discuss this matter with the Holy See. In no way am I implying that either the Holy See or we should ignore whatever real problems may exist—and admittedly there are some. But the way in which the response is given will make a big difference in the way it is received and accepted. On the basis of my experience, the vast majority of religious are generous and loyal. Those whose views are incompatible with the Church's understanding of religious life are a minority, and their position should not be permitted to determine how we will deal with the majority.

## ORDAINED MINISTRIES

There has been considerable discussion about the permanent diaconate. While the experience of many is positive, a number of concerns have been voiced. These include the identity of the deacon, his effective incorporation into the pastoral ministries of the diocese and its parishes, a danger of elitism and clericalism, the need for better screening and training, and so on. In light of such comments, I am convinced that we should seriously evaluate our experience with the permanent diaconate. Such a study would be helpful in determining future directions.

And now, priesthood. Priesthood is dear to all of us, and the decline in the number of candidates is of great concern. Archbishop Pilarczyk's paper highlights an important fact: Before there can be a turn-around, we must address the root causes of the present difficulty. It is neither possible nor necessary for me to give an overview of the situation. However, I do want to highlight several specific points.

1. We will not attract more candidates until we project an image of reasonably happy, healthy, satisfied men—men of deep faith who have made a firm commitment and show a certain enthusiasm for their ministry. As Archbishop Pilarczyk noted, it was such an image—such role modeling—that attracted young men before; without it, we cannot hope for much in the future.

2. To project such an image, several basic things are needed:

a. We must bring into clear focus our *identity* as priests. We need a theology of priesthood that is at once profound, understandable, and convincing. Who are we? What is our role and responsibility in the postconciliar Church? The introduction of lay ministries, which are so important and needed, was accompanied, unfortunately, by a blurring of roles, a tendency to telescope everything into a kind of common ministry. However, the identity of the priest, both theological and functional, cannot be achieved in isolation. It can only find its focus within the context of the ecclesial community and its mission to the world, and the vocation of the laity whom the priest is called to serve.

b. Along with priestly identity, we must deal with the issue of *celibacy*. Despite our pronouncements, support for celibacy continues to erode. While most people will admit that celibacy has value, a growing number see no reason to make it a precondition for priesthood. Archbishop Pilarczyk stated that this is not the first time that church leadership has had to deal with this matter. In a society where celibacy has become such a countercultural reality, what can we do to highlight its value both for the individual and the faith community? What personal qualities and attitudes are needed for one to live celibacy in a positive and fulfilling way? How do we develop an understanding of celibacy in a way that respects the authentic needs and expectations of both the individual and the faith community regarding interpersonal relationships and intimacy? It is not only a matter of the mind; it is, above all, a matter of the heart!

The development of a sound understanding and appreciation of celibacy should take place, as I indicated earlier, within the framework of a more positive theology of sexuality. This challenges us to promote mature psychosexual development in the initial and ongoing formation of our seminarians and priests.

c. The resolution of the identity and celibacy issues must be accompanied by a deep, mature spirituality. We need to develop a spirituality for priesthood—a spirituality that will give us the wisdom and strength not merely to cope with our lives and ministry but truly to grow and flourish. The development of such a spirituality has both an individual and a corporate dimension. In the final analysis, there is no substitute for personal piety, prudence, and discipline. But what must we do collectively? How do we assist and encourage one another? And how do we do all this, not in isolation from the people we serve, but together with them?

d. While we bishops are not the only actors, I am convinced that we are *key* actors in bringing all this about. First, our efforts will be credible and effective only if we ourselves are faith-filled ministers, totally committed to, comfortable with, and enthusiastic about the priesthood whose fullness we share. We will not be able to convince others if we have not first responded with all our mind and heart to the spirit of the Lord who animates every fiber of our being. Second, we must make available to our priests the spiritual and professional assistance they need. The allocation of adequate personnel and resources for this purpose is essential. Third, and perhaps most important of all, we must make ourselves personally available to our priests. This may be difficult in the larger dioceses (indeed, I know it is!), but it must be done. We must accompany our priests on their journey; we must share their agonies and ecstasies. In the final analysis, we are one with them.

Other important issues have emerged. For example, concern has been expressed about the process currently being used for laicization. Concern also has been expressed about the restrictions placed on priests who have been dispensed. Some feel that, assuming they have the necessary qualities and good will, those who are dispensed should be permitted to exercise any ecclesial ministry open to the laity. In any case, there is a need to relate with compassion to those who have left the active ministry. Some have asked whether, to alleviate pastoral needs, to ensure that the Eucharist is celebrated regularly in all parishes, consideration could be given to ordaining mature married men. These are sensitive questions. They must be considered in a context that takes into account the

Church's discipline, pastoral need, and our fidelity to the Holy See.

Given the insights that have emerged and the new directions that are called for, do we need to reexamine the focus of our diocesan vocation offices? While continuing to promote general vocational awareness and to nurture vocations, we must make sure that they also focus in a specific way on priesthood and religious life. It is crucial that the unique identity of the priest and religious not be blurred, and that those who seem to have the needed qualities and motivation be invited to consider seriously whether they have been called to the priesthood and religious life. This is particularly important for the diocesan priesthood.

As we discuss vocations, surely we must identify and address the problems if they are to be resolved. But let's not become captives of the problems. There is so much to say about priesthood that is positive. And, I am convinced that there are many who will respond to the call if we invite them. So let's go about our task with enthusiasm and confidence.

## CONCLUSION

May I suggest a vision of the Church that will provide us with the directions and motivation needed as we prepare for the third millenium of Christianity? In that vision, I see a community of faith over which the risen Lord truly presides. I see a community that continues to incarnate, in our contemporary context, the life and ministry of the first Christian community who "devoted themselves to the apostles instruction and the communal life, to the breaking of bread and the prayers" (Acts 3:42–43).

It is a community in which all members, in virtue of their incorporation into Christ through baptism and confirmation, witness to his saving deeds before the entire world and work for the emergence of the kingdom he proclaimed. It is a community whose designated ministers, whether ordained or lay, understand and accept their uniquely different but complementary and necessary roles, working together for the good of all.

It is a community whose faith in Jesus is far more compelling than any human consideration; one that honors truth more than idle speculation and bias; a community in which respect for persons rules out pettiness, unfairness, and mean-spiritedness, promoting instead candid dialogue, reconciliation, and unity. It is a community in which Jesus' love and mercy, his justice, his compassion and healing power are tangibly evident each day.

As bishops and pilgrims, the challenge is ours to help shape that kind of community for the Church in the United States. May God assist us in our effort!